W9-BMM-274

100 BEST
Bake Sale
RECIPES

Publications International, Ltd.
Favorite Brand Name Recipes at www.fbnr.com

Pictured on the front cover: Morning Muffins with Blueberries *(page 30)*.
Pictured on the back cover *(clockwise from top left):* Mom's Pumpkin Pie *(page 154)*, Basic Oatmeal Cookies *(page 18)*, Blueberry Yogurt Cake *(page 48)* and Toll House® Famous Fudge *(page 128)*.

ISBN-13: 978-1-4127-2545-3
ISBN-10: 1-4127-2545-3

Library of Congress Control Number: 2007920131

Manufactured in China.

8 7 6 5 4 3 2 1

Microwave Cooking: Microwave ovens vary in wattage. Use the cooking times as guidelines and check for doneness before adding more time.

Preparation/Cooking Times: Preparation times are based on the approximate amount of time required to assemble the recipe before cooking, baking, chilling or serving. These times include preparation steps such as measuring, chopping and mixing. The fact that some preparations and cooking can be done simultaneously is taken into account. Preparation of optional ingredients and serving suggestions is not included.

Table of Contents

Cookie Jar Explosion

Apple Cinnamon Chunkies

1 package (18 ounces) refrigerated oatmeal raisin cookie dough
1 cup chopped dried apples
½ cup cinnamon baking chips
½ teaspoon apple pie spice*

*You may substitute ¼ teaspoon ground cinnamon, ⅛ teaspoon ground nutmeg and pinch of ground allspice or ground cloves for ½ teaspoon apple pie spice.

1. Let dough stand at room temperature about 15 minutes. Preheat oven to 350°F. Lightly grease cookie sheets.

2. Combine dough, apples, cinnamon chips and apple pie spice in large bowl; stir until well blended. Drop dough by rounded tablespoonfuls 2 inches apart onto prepared cookie sheets.

3. Bake 10 to 12 minutes or until golden brown. Cool on cookie sheets 2 to 3 minutes. Remove to wire racks; cool completely.

Makes 2 dozen cookies

__Clockwise from top left:__ Apple Cinnamon Chunkies, Choco-Orange Macadamia Cookies (page 12), Pistachio Cookies (page 20) and Snickerdoodles (page 21).

Island Cookies

1⅔ cups all-purpose flour
¾ teaspoon baking powder
½ teaspoon baking soda
½ teaspoon salt
¾ cup (1½ sticks) butter, softened
¾ cup packed brown sugar
⅓ cup granulated sugar
1 teaspoon vanilla extract
1 egg
1¾ cups (11.5-ounce package) NESTLÉ® TOLL HOUSE® Milk
    Chocolate Morsels
1 cup flaked coconut, toasted, if desired
1 cup chopped walnuts

PREHEAT oven to 375°F.

COMBINE flour, baking powder, baking soda and salt in small bowl. Beat butter, brown sugar, granulated sugar and vanilla extract in large mixer bowl until creamy. Beat in egg. Gradually beat in flour mixture. Stir in morsels, coconut and nuts. Drop by slightly rounded tablespoon onto ungreased baking sheets.

BAKE for 8 to 11 minutes or until edges are lightly browned. Cool on baking sheets for 2 minutes; remove to wire racks to cool completely.

Makes about 3 dozen cookies

Note: NESTLÉ® TOLL HOUSE® Semi-Sweet Chocolate Morsels, Semi-Sweet Chocolate Mini Morsels, Premier White Morsels or Butterscotch Flavored Morsels can be substituted for the Milk Chocolate Morsels.

Island Cookies

Classic Chocolate Chip Cookies

1¼ cups all-purpose flour
½ teaspoon salt
½ teaspoon baking soda
½ cup (1 stick) butter, softened
½ cup granulated sugar
¼ cup packed light brown sugar
1 egg, lightly beaten
1 teaspoon vanilla
1 cup semisweet chocolate chips
½ cup coarsely chopped walnuts (optional)

1. Preheat oven to 350°F. Lightly grease cookie sheets; set aside. Combine flour, salt and baking soda in medium bowl.

2. Beat butter and sugars in large bowl until light and fluffy. Add egg and vanilla; beat until well blended. Add flour mixture; beat just until blended. Stir in chocolate chips and walnuts, if desired.

3. Drop dough by tablespoonfuls 2 inches apart onto prepared cookie sheets.

4. Bake 10 to 12 minutes or until edges are lightly browned. Cool on cookie sheets 1 minute. Remove to wire racks; cool completely.

Makes about 3 dozen cookies

Helpful Hint

Tip

Chocolate chip cookies freeze very well. After cooling completely, place cookies in an airtight container or resealable food storage bag. When ready to eat or sell, just allow cookies to come to room temperature.

Classic Chocolate Chip Cookies

Toasted Almond and Cranberry Biscotti

4 tablespoons (½ stick) butter, softened, divided
1 cup whole blanched almonds
2½ cups all-purpose flour
1 cup granulated sugar
1 teaspoon baking powder
½ teaspoon baking soda
2 eggs
1 teaspoon almond extract
¼ teaspoon vanilla
½ cup milk
1 cup dried cranberries
2 tablespoons packed brown sugar

1. Preheat oven to 350°F. Lightly grease cookie sheets.

2. Melt 1 tablespoon butter in small skillet. Remove from heat; add almonds. Stir gently to coat almonds. Place in single layer on ungreased baking pan. Bake 8 to 10 minutes or until golden brown and fragrant, stirring frequently. Almonds can easily burn so watch carefully. Immediately remove almonds from pan; cool completely.

3. Stir together flour, sugar, baking powder and baking soda in large bowl. Add eggs, almond extract, vanilla and 2 tablespoons butter; beat with electric mixer on medium-low speed until soft dough forms. Continue beating, adding milk 1 tablespoon at a time, just until dough becomes smooth. Add almonds and cranberries. Knead dough gently in bowl until well blended. Transfer dough to floured surface; divide in half. Shape each half into 12×2-inch loaf on prepared cookie sheet.

4. Bake about 15 minutes or until lightly browned on top. Remove from oven and roll logs over exposing unbrowned bottoms. Return to oven; bake 15 minutes more or until evenly brown all over (loaf will sound hollow when tapped). Cool on wire rack 12 or 15 minutes or until cool enough to handle with bare hands.

5. While still warm, slice diagonally into pieces about ½ inch thick. Place slices on ungreased cookie sheets. Bake 10 minutes more on each side or until brown. Remove to wire racks; cool completely.

6. Melt remaining 1 tablespoon butter with brown sugar in small skillet over medium-high heat. Cook and stir until dark golden brown. Drizzle in thin ribbons over cookies.   *Makes about 4 dozen cookies*

Toasted Almond and Cranberry Biscotti

Choco-Orange Macadamia Cookies

1 cup raw macadamia nuts
2 cups plus 1 tablespoon all-purpose flour
½ teaspoon baking powder
½ teaspoon salt
¾ cup (1½ sticks) butter, melted and cooled
1 cup packed light brown sugar
6 tablespoons granulated sugar
2 teaspoons grated orange peel
2 teaspoons vanilla
1 egg
1 egg yolk
1 cup semisweet chocolate chips
½ cup flaked coconut

1. Preheat oven to 350°F. Place macadamia nuts in shallow ungreased baking pan. Bake 6 to 8 minutes or until golden brown and fragrant, stirring frequently. (Nuts can easily burn so watch carefully.) Cool completely. Coarsely chop nuts; set aside.

2. Combine flour, baking powder and salt in medium bowl.

3. Beat butter, sugars, orange peel and vanilla in large bowl with electric mixer at medium speed until creamy. Beat in egg and egg yolk until fluffy. Gradually add flour mixture, beating until just blended. Stir in nuts, chocolate chips and coconut.

4. Drop dough by rounded tablespoonfuls 2 inches apart onto ungreased cookie sheets. Bake 10 to 12 minutes or until edges are just brown but centers are pale. Cool on cookie sheets 1 minute. Remove to wire racks; cool completely. Store in airtight container.

Makes about 3 dozen cookies

Fruity Coconut Oatmeal Cookies

1 recipe Basic Oatmeal Cookies (page 18)
¼ teaspoon ground cinnamon
½ cup finely diced dried mango
½ cup finely diced dried apple
½ cup finely diced dried cherries
3 cups shredded sweetened coconut, divided

1. Preheat oven to 350°F. Line cookie sheets with parchment paper.

2. Prepare dough for Basic Oatmeal Cookies, adding cinnamon with salt.

3. Add mango, apple, cherries and ½ cup coconut.

4. Spread remaining 2½ cups coconut on plate. Drop dough by rounded tablespoonfuls into coconut and roll to coat.

5. Place on prepared cookie sheets. Bake 15 to 17 minutes or until puffed and golden. Cool on cookie sheet 5 minutes. Remove to wire racks; cool completely.   *Makes about 40 cookies*

Tip: If desired, substitute 1 bag (6 ounces) of tropical medley dried chopped fruit for the mango, apple and cherries.

Cornmeal Butter Cookies

   2 cups corn flour
   ½ cup cornmeal, not coarse-ground
   ½ teaspoon salt
   1 cup (2 sticks) unsalted butter, softened
   ⅓ cup plus 2 tablespoons sugar, divided
   1 egg
   ¼ cup pure maple syrup

1. Preheat oven to 350°F. Line 2 cookie sheets with parchment paper. Combine corn flour, cornmeal and salt in medium bowl; set aside.

2. Beat butter and ⅓ cup sugar in large bowl with electric mixer at medium-high speed. Beat in egg and maple syrup until combined. Add corn flour mixture ½ cup at a time, mixing well. Refrigerate dough 30 minutes.

3. Shape dough into 1-inch balls. Place 1 inch apart on prepared cookie sheets. Flatten dough to ½-inch thickness using the bottom of a glass dipped in remaining 2 tablespoons sugar.

4. Bake for 12 to 14 minutes or until golden brown around the edges. Cool on cookie sheets 2 minutes. Remove cookies to wire rack; cool completely.
                           Makes 4 dozen cookies

Dark Cocoa Spice Cookies

Dough
2½ cups all-purpose flour
½ cup unsweetened Dutch process cocoa powder
1 teaspoon ground cinnamon
1 teaspoon ground cardamom
½ teaspoon baking soda
¼ teaspoon salt
1 cup (2 sticks) unsalted butter, softened
1½ cups packed dark brown sugar
2 egg yolks
1 teaspoon coconut extract
Demerara sugar or decorating sugar

Royal Icing
1 large egg white
1¼ cups sifted powdered sugar
Pinch cream of tartar

1. Sift together flour, cocoa, cinnamon, cardamom, baking soda, and salt in medium bowl; set aside.

2. Beat butter and brown sugar in large bowl with electric mixer at medium speed until light and fluffy. Beat in egg yolks and coconut extract. Add sifted flour mixture and mix well.

3. Gather dough into ball and divide into 4 equal pieces. Shape each piece into 6-inch-long log. Wrap in plastic wrap and refrigerate 3 to 4 hours or until firm.

4. Preheat oven to 325°F. Line cookie sheets with parchment paper. Slice each log into 16 cookies. Place 1 inch apart on cookie sheets and bake 12 minutes. Cool on cookie sheets 5 minutes. Remove to wire racks; cool completely.

5. For royal icing, beat egg white, powdered sugar and cream of tartar in small bowl with electric mixer at medium speed until thick and smooth. Cover icing with damp cloth during use to prevent icing from drying.

6. Use small paint brush to brush edges of cooled cookies with royal icing, then roll edges in demerara sugar before icing hardens.

Makes about 60 cookies

Tip: Keep your paint brush in the kitchen where it belongs and out of the kids' art projects by writing "kitchen only" on the wooden handle in marker.

Dark Cocoa Spice Cookies

Mini Apricot-Filled Pinwheels

  2 cups coarsely chopped dried apricots
  ½ cup apricot preserves
  ½ cup golden raisins
  ¾ cup water
  1 teaspoon ground cinnamon
  2 packages (12.4 ounces) refrigerated cinnamon rolls with icing

1. Combine apricots, preserves, raisins, water and cinnamon in heavy saucepan; cook and stir over medium heat. Bring to a boil, then lower heat. Simmer 10 to 15 minutes or until fruit is softened. Cool 30 minutes, then process in food processor or blender, pulsing until finely chopped. Cool 30 minutes more.

2. Roll out cinnamon rolls on floured cutting board until thin, forming 5-inch circles. Spread each circle with 2 tablespoons apricot filling. Roll up each circle jelly-roll style. Place rolls in freezer for 30 minutes or until firm enough to cut.

3. Preheat oven to 350°F. Line cookie sheets with parchment paper. Slice rolls into ½-inch cookies. Shape into round cookies and place cookies 1 inch apart on cookie sheets; flatten slightly. Bake 7 to 9 minutes or until lightly browned.

4. Cool on cookie sheets 2 minutes. Remove to wire racks; cool completely. Drizzle cookies with cinnamon roll icing.   *Makes about 96 mini cookies*

Tip: Try substituting your favorite fruit preserves for the apricot. Apple jelly or red currant preserves would be delicious.

Mini Apricot-Filled Pinwheels

Basic Oatmeal Cookies

1⅓ **cups all-purpose flour**
¾ **teaspoon baking soda**
½ **teaspoon baking powder**
½ **teaspoon salt**
2 **cups old-fashioned oats**
¾ **cup (1½ sticks) unsalted butter, softened**
1 **cup packed light brown sugar**
¼ **cup granulated sugar**
1 **egg**
1 **tablespoon honey**
1 **teaspoon vanilla**

1. Preheat oven to 350°F. Line cookie sheets with parchment paper. Combine flour, baking soda, baking powder and salt in large bowl. Stir in oats; set aside.

2. Combine butter and sugars in large bowl; beat with electric mixer at medium speed until well blended. Beat on high speed until light and fluffy. Scrape down bowl. Add egg, honey and vanilla; beat on medium speed until well blended. Gradually add flour mixture, about ½ cup at a time, scraping sides of bowl occasionally. Do not overwork dough.

3. Drop dough by rounded tablespoonfuls 2 inches apart onto prepared cookie sheets. Bake one pan at a time, 11 to 13 minutes, or until puffed and golden. Do not overbake. Cool on cookie sheets 5 minutes. Remove to wire racks; cool completely. *Makes 3 dozen cookies*

Helpful Hint

Tip

This basic dough recipe lets you use your imagination to create fun variations. Add dried fruit, chocolate chips or even your favorite chopped candy. Try spreading ice cream between two cookies for a homemade ice cream sandwich.

Basic Oatmeal Cookies

Pistachio Cookies

 1 cup (2 sticks) butter, softened
 ¾ cup granulated sugar
 ¼ cup packed brown sugar
 ¼ cup unsweetened cocoa powder (optional)
 1 teaspoon baking powder
 ¼ teaspoon ground nutmeg
 1 egg
 1½ teaspoons vanilla
 2 cups all-purpose flour
 1 cup coarsely chopped pistachio nuts

1. Preheat oven to 350°F. Line cookie sheets with parchment paper.

2. Beat butter, sugars, cocoa, if desired, baking powder and nutmeg in large bowl with electric mixer at medium speed until creamy. Add egg and vanilla; beat until fluffy.

3. Stir in flour just until moist. Fold in nuts. (Do not overmix.) Cover bowl with plastic wrap or damp cloth; refrigerate 1 hour.

4. Shape tablespoonfuls of dough into balls. Place 4 inches apart on prepared cookie sheets. Bake 10 to 12 minutes or until set. Remove to wire rack; cool completely.   *Makes about 2 dozen cookies*

One-Bite Pineapple Chewies

 ½ cup whipping cream
 ¼ cup sugar
 ⅛ teaspoon salt
 1 cup finely chopped dried pineapple
 ½ cup slivered and chopped almonds
 ¼ cup mini semisweet chocolate chips
 ¼ cup all-purpose flour

1. Preheat oven to 350°F. Line 2 cookie sheets with parchment paper.

2. Stir together cream, sugar and salt in large bowl until sugar dissolves. Stir in pineapple, almonds and chocolate chips. Stir in flour.

3. Drop batter by rounded teaspoonfuls 1 inch apart onto prepared cookie sheets. Bake 13 to 15 minutes or until cookies are golden at edges. Cool on cookie sheets 2 minutes. Remove to wire rack; cool completely.

Makes about 4½ dozen cookies

Snickerdoodles

 ¾ cup sugar plus 1 tablespoon sugar, divided
 2 teaspoons cinnamon, divided
1⅓ cups all-purpose flour
 1 teaspoon cream of tartar
 ½ teaspoon baking soda
 ½ cup (1 stick) butter
 1 egg
 1 package (6 ounces) cinnamon baking chips
 1 cup raisins (optional)

1. Preheat oven to 400°F. Combine 1 tablespoon sugar and 1 teaspoon cinnamon in small bowl; set aside.

2. Combine flour, remaining 1 teaspoon cinnamon, cream of tartar and soda in medium bowl. Beat remaining ¾ cup sugar and butter in large bowl with electric mixer at medium speed until creamy. Beat in egg. Gradually add flour mixture to sugar mixture, beating at low speed until stiff dough forms. Stir in cinnamon chips and raisins, if desired.

3. Roll dough into 1-inch balls; roll in cinnamon-sugar mixture. Place on ungreased cookie sheets.

4. Bake 10 minutes or until firm in center. *Do not overbake*. Remove to wire racks; cool completely.

Makes about 3 dozen cookies

Mocha Dots

1 tablespoon instant coffee granules
2 tablespoons hot water
1½ cups all-purpose flour
¼ cup unsweetened cocoa powder
½ teaspoon salt
½ teaspoon baking soda
½ cup (1 stick) butter, softened
½ cup granulated sugar
¼ cup packed light brown sugar
1 egg, lightly beaten
1 teaspoon vanilla
Chocolate nonpareil candies (about 1-inch in diameter)

1. Preheat oven to 350°F. Lightly grease cookie sheets; set aside. Dissolve instant coffee granules in hot water; let cool slightly. Combine flour, cocoa, salt and baking soda in medium bowl.

2. Beat butter and sugars in large bowl with electric mixer at medium speed until light and fluffy. Add egg, coffee mixture and vanilla; beat until well blended. Add flour mixture; beat until well blended.

3. Shape dough by level teaspoonfuls into balls; place 2 inches apart on prepared cookie sheets. Gently press 1 candy onto center of each ball. (Do not press candies too far into dough balls. Cookies will spread around candies as they bake.)

4. Bake 7 to 8 minutes or until set and no longer shiny. Cool on cookie sheets 2 minutes. Remove to wire racks; cool completely.

Makes about 6½ dozen cookies

Mocha Dots

Hungarian Lemon Poppy Seed Cookies

Cookies
  ⅔ **cup granulated sugar**
  ½ **cup (1 stick) butter, softened**
  1 egg
  2 teaspoons grated lemon peel
1¼ **cups all-purpose flour**
  ½ **teaspoon baking soda**
  ¼ **teaspoon salt**
  1 tablespoon poppy seeds

Glaze
  1 cup powdered sugar
  2 tablespoons lemon juice

1. Preheat oven to 350°F.

2. For cookies, beat granulated sugar and butter in large bowl of electric mixer at medium speed until creamy. Beat in egg and lemon peel. Combine flour, baking soda and salt in small bowl; gradually add to butter mixture. Beat in poppy seeds on low speed.

3. Drop dough by heaping teaspoonfuls 2 inches apart onto ungreased cookie sheets. Bake 11 to 12 minutes or until edges are lightly browned. Cool on cookie sheets 1 minute. Remove to wire racks; cool completely.

4. For glaze, combine powdered sugar and lemon juice in small bowl; mix well. Drizzle glaze over cookies; let stand until glaze is set, about 20 minutes. *Makes about 2 dozen cookies*

Hungarian Lemon Poppy Seed Cookies

Peanut Butter and Milk Chocolate Chip Studded Oatmeal Cookies

1 cup (2 sticks) butter or margarine, softened
1 cup packed light brown sugar
⅓ cup granulated sugar
2 eggs
1½ teaspoons vanilla extract
1½ cups all-purpose flour
1 teaspoon baking soda
½ teaspoon salt
½ teaspoon ground cinnamon (optional)
2½ cups quick-cooking oats
1 cup HERSHEY'S® Milk Chocolate Chips
1 cup REESE'S® Peanut Butter Chips

1. Heat oven to 350°F.

2. Beat butter, brown sugar and granulated sugar in bowl until creamy. Add eggs and vanilla; beat well. Combine flour, baking soda, salt and cinnamon, if desired; add to butter mixture, beating well. Stir in oats, milk chocolate chips and peanut butter chips (batter will be stiff). Drop by rounded teaspoons onto ungreased cookie sheet.

3. Bake 10 to 12 minutes or until lightly browned. Cool 1 minute; remove from cookie sheet to wire rack. *Makes about 4 dozen bars*

Bar Variation: Spread batter into lightly greased 13×9×2-inch baking pan or 15½×10½×1-inch jelly-roll pan. Bake at 350°F. for 20 to 25 minutes or until golden brown. Cool; cut into bars. Makes about 3 dozen bars.

Peanut Butter and Milk Chocolate Chip Studded
Oatmeal Cookies

Breakfast Baked Goods

Pumpkin Raisin Bread

- ⅓ cup butter, softened
- 1⅓ cups EQUAL® Sugar Lite™
- ¾ cup canned pumpkin
- 2 eggs
- ⅓ cup 2% milk
- 1 teaspoon vanilla extract
- 1½ cups self-rising flour
- ½ teaspoon ground cinnamon
- ½ teaspoon ground nutmeg
- ⅓ cup raisins
- 1½ tablespoons self-rising flour

Beat butter and EQUAL® Sugar Lite™ until well blended. Mix in pumpkin, eggs, milk and vanilla until combined.

Combine 1½ cups self-rising flour, cinnamon and nutmeg. Mix into pumpkin batter until well blended. Combine raisins and 1½ tablespoons flour. Fold into pumpkin mixture. Preheat oven to 350°F.

Spoon mixture into a 9×5-inch loaf pan well sprayed with cooking spray. Bake 50 to 55 minutes or until a wooden pick inserted near center comes out clean. Cool in pan on wire rack 10 minutes. Remove bread and cool completely. *Makes 16 servings*

Clockwise from top left: Pumpkin Raisin Bread, Cinnamon Cereal Crispies (page 42), Cinnamini Buns (page 47) and Orange Coffee Cake with Streusel Topping (page 37).

Morning Muffins with Blueberries

½ cup plus 1 tablespoon sugar, divided
⅛ teaspoon ground cinnamon
1¾ cups all-purpose flour
2 teaspoons baking powder
½ teaspoon salt
½ cup milk
¼ cup vegetable oil
1 egg
1 teaspoon vanilla
1 teaspoon grated orange peel
1 cup fresh or frozen blueberries, thawed and dried

1. Preheat oven to 400°F. Grease 12 standard (2½-inch) muffin cups or line with paper baking cups. Combine 1 tablespoon sugar and cinnamon in small bowl; set aside.

2. Combine flour, remaining ½ cup sugar, baking powder and salt in large bowl. Beat milk, oil, egg, vanilla and orange peel in small bowl until blended. Make a well in center of flour mixture; stir in milk mixture just until moistened. Fold in blueberries. Spoon evenly into prepared muffin cups, filling about two-thirds full.

3. Bake 15 to 18 minutes or until toothpick inserted into centers comes out clean. Immediately sprinkle cinnamon-sugar mixture over hot muffins. Transfer to wire racks. Serve warm. *Makes 12 muffins*

Tip: For muffins with larger tops, fill the muffin cups almost full and bake at 400°F until a toothpick inserted into the centers comes out clean. Proceed as directed above. (The recipe will make about 8 big-top muffins.)

Morning Muffins with Blueberries

Apple Crumb Coffeecake

2¼ cups all-purpose flour, divided
½ cup sugar
1 envelope FLEISCHMANN'S® RapidRise™ Yeast
½ teaspoon salt
¼ cup water
¼ cup milk
⅓ cup butter or margarine
2 eggs
2 cooking apples, cored and sliced
   Crumb Topping (recipe follows)

In large bowl, combine 1 cup flour, sugar, undissolved yeast and salt. Heat water, milk and butter until very warm (120° to 130°F). Gradually add to dry ingredients. Beat 2 minutes at medium speed of electric mixer, scraping bowl occasionally. Add eggs and ½ cup flour. Beat 2 minutes at high speed, scraping bowl occasionally. Stir in remaining ¾ cup flour to make stiff batter. Spread evenly in greased 9-inch square pan. Arrange apple slices evenly over batter. Sprinkle Crumb Topping over apples. Cover; let rise in warm, draft-free place until doubled in size, about 1 hour.

Bake at 375°F for 35 to 40 minutes or until done. Cool in pan 10 minutes. Remove from pan; cool on wire rack.   *Makes 1 (9-inch) cake*

Crumb Topping: Combine ⅓ cup sugar, ¼ cup all-purpose flour, 3 tablespoons cold butter or margarine and 1 teaspoon ground cinnamon, using a pastry blender to mix all ingredients until coarse crumbs form.

Apple Crumb Coffeecake

Baked Banana Doughnuts

2 ripe bananas, mashed
2 egg whites
1 tablespoon vegetable oil
1 cup packed brown sugar
1½ cups all-purpose flour
¾ cup whole wheat flour
2 teaspoons baking powder
½ teaspoon baking soda
¼ teaspoon pumpkin pie spice
1 tablespoon granulated sugar
2 tablespoons chopped walnuts (optional)

Preheat oven to 425°F. Spray baking sheet with nonstick cooking spray. Beat bananas, egg whites, oil and brown sugar in large bowl or food processor. Add flours, baking powder, baking soda and pumpkin pie spice. Mix until well blended. Let stand for five minutes for dough to rise. Scoop out heaping tablespoonfuls of dough onto prepared baking sheet. Using thin rubber spatula or butter knife round out doughnut hole in center of dough (if dough sticks to knife or spatula, spray with cooking spray). With spatula, smooth outside edges of dough into round doughnut shape. Repeat until all dough is used. Sprinkle with granulated sugar and walnuts, if desired. Bake 6 to 10 minutes or until tops are golden.   *Makes about 22 doughnuts*

Variation: Use 8 ounces solid pack pumpkin instead of bananas to make pumpkin doughnuts.

Favorite recipe from **The Sugar Association, Inc.**

Baked Banana Doughnuts

Triple-Chocolate Dippers

1 cup (2 sticks) butter, softened
½ cup packed brown sugar
⅓ cup granulated sugar
1 egg
1⅔ cup all-purpose flour
¼ cup unsweetened cocoa
¼ teaspoon baking powder
¼ teaspoon baking soda
¼ teaspoon salt
1 cup semisweet chocolate chips
½ cup chopped walnuts

Glaze
1 cup semisweet chocolate chips
1 tablespoon vegetable oil

1. Preheat oven to 400°F. Line two cookie sheets with parchment paper. Beat butter, brown sugar and granulated sugar in large bowl with electric mixer at medium-high speed. Beat in egg until blended.

2. Combine flour, cocoa, baking powder, baking soda and salt in a small bowl. Add to mixer, ¼ cup at a time, until well blended. Stir in chocolate chips and walnuts.

3. Drop dough, 2 tablespoonfuls at a time, onto prepared cookie sheets and shape into a log about 3 inches long and 1 inch wide; leave about 1½ inches between logs. Bake for 14 to 15 minutes or until cookies are firm. Cool on cookie sheets 2 minutes. Remove to wire racks; cool completely.

4. For glaze, melt chocolate chips in top of double boiler; stir in oil. Drizzle glaze over cookies using a fork. Refrigerate cookies to set glaze quickly.

Makes about 2 dozen cookies

Note: If dough gets too soft to handle, chill for 30 minutes, then shape into logs.

Orange Coffeecake with Streusel Topping

1 package (about 19 ounces) cinnamon swirl muffin mix
1 egg
1 teaspoon grated orange peel
¾ cup orange juice
½ cup pecan pieces

1. Preheat oven to 400°F. Grease 9-inch square baking pan; set aside.

2. Place muffin mix in large bowl; break up any lumps. Add egg, orange peel and juice; stir until just moistened. (Batter will be slightly lumpy.) Spoon batter into prepared pan. Knead cinnamon swirl packet 10 seconds. Cut off 1 end of packet; squeeze contents over batter. Swirl into batter using knife or spatula; do not mix in completely. Sprinkle with topping packet and pecans.

3. Bake 23 to 25 minutes or until toothpick inserted into center comes out almost clean. Cool in pan on wire rack 15 minutes.   *Makes 9 servings*

Strawberry Muffins

1¼ cups all-purpose flour
1 cup uncooked old-fashioned oats
½ cup sugar
2½ teaspoons baking powder
½ teaspoon salt
1 cup milk
½ cup (1 stick) butter, melted
1 egg, beaten
1 teaspoon vanilla
1 cup chopped fresh strawberries

1. Preheat oven to 425°F. Grease 12 standard (2½-inch) muffin pan cups or line with paper baking cups.

2. Combine flour, oats, sugar, baking powder and salt in large bowl. Combine milk, butter, egg and vanilla in small bowl until well blended; stir into flour mixture just until moistened. Fold in strawberries. Spoon into prepared muffin cups, filling about two-thirds full.

3. Bake 15 to 18 minutes or until lightly browned and toothpick inserted into centers comes out clean. Remove from pan. Cool on wire rack 10 minutes. Serve warm or cool completely.   *Makes 12 muffins*

Bacon Cheddar Muffins

2 cups all-purpose flour
¾ cup sugar
2 teaspoons baking powder
½ teaspoon baking soda
½ teaspoon salt
¾ cup plus 2 tablespoons milk
⅓ cup butter, melted
1 egg, lightly beaten
1 cup (4 ounces) shredded Cheddar cheese
½ cup crisp-cooked and crumbled bacon (about 6 slices)

1. Preheat oven to 350°F. Grease 12 standard (2½-inch) muffin cups or line with paper baking cups.

2. Combine flour, sugar, baking powder, baking soda and salt in medium bowl. Combine milk, butter and egg in small bowl; mix well. Add milk mixture to flour mixture; stir just until blended. Gently stir in cheese and bacon. Spoon evenly into prepared muffin cups, filling three-quarters full.

3. Bake 15 to 20 minutes or until toothpick inserted into centers comes out clean. Cool muffins in pan 2 minutes; remove to wire rack. Serve warm or at room temperature.   *Makes 12 muffins*

Helpful Hint

While gathering your other ingredients, try cooking the bacon in the microwave. Place strips on a paper towel-lined plate and cook according to package directions. When bacon is cool it will be very easy to crumble.

Bacon Cheddar Muffins

Cherry Banana Bread

1 (10-ounce) jar maraschino cherries
1¾ cups all-purpose flour
2 teaspoons baking powder
½ teaspoon salt
⅔ cup firmly packed brown sugar
⅓ cup butter or margarine, softened
2 eggs
1 cup mashed ripe bananas
½ cup chopped macadamia nuts or walnuts

Drain maraschino cherries, reserving 2 tablespoons juice. Cut cherries into quarters; set aside. Combine flour, baking powder and salt; set aside.

Combine brown sugar, butter, eggs and reserved cherry juice in a large bowl. Mix with an electric mixer at medium speed 3 to 4 minutes, or until well mixed. Add flour mixture and mashed bananas alternately, beginning and ending with flour mixture. Stir in drained cherries and nuts. Lightly spray a 9×5×3-inch baking pan with nonstick cooking spray. Spread batter evenly in pan.

Bake in a preheated 350°F oven 1 hour, or until golden brown and wooden pick inserted near center comes out clean. Remove from pan; let cool on wire rack. To store, wrap bread in plastic wrap.

Makes 1 loaf, about 16 slices

Favorite recipe from **Cherry Marketing Institute**

Cherry Banana Bread

Jammy Wedges

1 package (18 ounces) refrigerated sugar cookie dough
¼ cup granulated sugar
1 egg
3 tablespoons blackberry jam

1. Let dough stand at room temperature about 15 minutes. Preheat oven to 350°F. Lightly grease 9-inch glass pie plate; line bottom of plate with waxed paper.

2. Combine dough, granulated sugar and egg in large bowl; beat until well blended. (Dough will be sticky.) Spread dough in prepared pie plate; smooth top. Dot top of dough with jam. Swirl jam into dough using tip of knife.

3. Bake 30 to 35 minutes or until edges are light brown and center is set. Cool 5 minutes in pie plate on wire rack. Cut into wedges just before serving. *Makes 8 to 10 servings*

Cinnamon Cereal Crispies

½ cup granulated sugar
2 teaspoons ground cinnamon, divided
1 package (18¼ ounces) white cake mix with pudding in the mix
⅓ cup vegetable oil
1 egg
2 cups crisp rice cereal
1 cup cornflakes
1 cup raisins
1 cup chopped nuts (optional)

1. Preheat oven to 350°F. Lightly spray cookie sheets with nonstick cooking spray. Combine sugar and 1 teaspoon cinnamon in small bowl.

2. Beat cake mix, ½ cup water, oil, egg and remaining 1 teaspoon cinnamon in large bowl with electric mixer at medium speed 1 minute. Gently stir in rice cereal, cornflakes, raisins and nuts, if desired, until well blended.

3. Drop batter by rounded tablespoonfuls 2 inches apart onto prepared cookie sheets. Sprinkle lightly with one half of cinnamon-sugar mixture.

4. Bake about 15 minutes or until lightly browned. Sprinkle cookies with remaining cinnamon-sugar mixture after baking. Remove to wire racks; cool completely. *Makes about 5 dozen cookies*

Jammy Wedges

Confetti Scones

  2 teaspoons olive oil
⅓ cup minced red bell pepper
⅓ cup minced green bell pepper
½ teaspoon dried thyme
  1 cup all-purpose flour
¼ cup whole wheat flour
1½ teaspoons baking powder
½ teaspoon baking soda
½ teaspoon sugar
¼ teaspoon ground red pepper
⅛ teaspoon salt
⅓ cup sour cream
⅓ cup milk
  2 tablespoons minced scallions
¼ cup grated Parmesan cheese
    Nonstick cooking spray

1. Preheat oven to 400°F. Line baking sheet with parchment paper; set aside.

2. Heat oil in small skillet. Add bell peppers and thyme; cook and stir 5 minutes or until tender. Set aside. Combine all-purpose flour, whole wheat flour, baking powder, baking soda, sugar, ground red pepper and salt in mixing bowl. Stir well. Add sour cream, milk and scallions. Mix to form a sticky dough. Stir in cheese (do not overmix).

3. Drop dough by rounded tablespoonfuls onto prepared baking sheet. Spray tops lightly with nonstick cooking spray. Place in oven and immediately turn oven heat down to 375°F. Bake 13 to 15 minutes or until golden. Remove to wire rack to cool. *Makes 24 scones*

Confetti Scones

Jumbo Streusel-Topped Raspberry Muffins

2¼ cups all-purpose flour, divided
¼ cup packed brown sugar
2 tablespoons cold butter
¾ cup granulated sugar
2 teaspoons baking powder
½ teaspoon baking soda
½ teaspoon salt
½ teaspoon grated lemon peel
¾ cup plus 2 tablespoons milk
⅓ cup butter, melted
1 egg, beaten
2 cups fresh or frozen raspberries (do not thaw)

1. Preheat oven to 350°F. Grease 6 jumbo (3½-inch) muffin cups.

2. To prepare topping, combine ¼ cup flour and brown sugar in small bowl. Cut in 2 tablespoons butter with pastry blender or two knives until mixture forms coarse crumbs.

3. Reserve ¼ cup flour; set aside. Combine remaining 1¾ cups flour, granulated sugar, baking powder, baking soda, salt and lemon peel in medium bowl. Combine milk, melted butter and egg in small bowl.

4. Add milk mixture to flour mixture; stir until almost blended. Toss frozen raspberries with reserved flour in medium bowl just until coated; gently fold raspberries into muffin batter. Spoon batter into prepared muffin cups, filling three-quarters full. Sprinkle with reserved topping.

5. Bake 25 to 30 minutes or until toothpick inserted into centers comes out clean. Cool in pan 2 minutes; remove to wire rack. Serve warm or at room temperature. *Makes 6 jumbo muffins*

Variation: For smaller muffins, spoon batter into 12 standard (2½-inch) greased or paper-lined muffin cups. Bake at 350°F 21 to 24 minutes or until toothpick inserted into centers comes out clean. Makes 12 muffins.

Breakfast Cookies

2 cups all-purpose flour
1 teaspoon baking powder
1 teaspoon ground cinnamon
½ teaspoon baking soda
½ teaspoon salt
¾ cup (1½ sticks) unsalted butter, softened
1 cup vanilla-flavored soy milk
2 eggs
¼ cup honey
2 cups crunchy lightly-sweetened, high-protein, high-fiber cereal
¾ cup raisins

1. Preheat oven to 350°F. Line two cookie sheets with parchment paper. Combine flour, baking powder, cinnamon, baking soda and salt in medium bowl.

2. Beat butter in large bowl with electric mixer at medium-high speed. Add soy milk, eggs and honey; beat until blended. Gradually add flour mixture until blended. Fold in cereal and raisins.

3. Drop by 2 tablespoonfuls onto prepared cookie sheets. Bake 18 to 20 minutes or until golden brown. Cool on cookie sheets 1 minute. Remove to wire racks; cool completely. *Makes 2½ dozen cookies*

Cinnamini Buns

1 can (8 ounces) refrigerated crescent roll dough
1 tablespoon butter, melted
2 tablespoons packed brown sugar
½ teaspoon ground cinnamon
½ cup powdered sugar
1 tablespoon milk

1. Preheat oven to 375°F. Generously grease large baking sheet. Unroll dough and separate into two long (12×4-inch) rectangles; press perforations to seal. Brush dough with butter; sprinkle with brown sugar and cinnamon. Roll up each rectangle tightly starting from long side; pinch edges to seal. Cut each roll into 12 (1-inch) slices. Place slices, cut sides up, about 1½ inches apart on prepared baking sheet.

2. Bake 10 minutes or until golden brown. Remove to wire rack. Blend powdered sugar and milk in small bowl until smooth. Drizzle glaze over top. *Makes 2 dozen mini cinnamon buns*

Blueberry Yogurt Cake

1 cup applesauce
½ cup granulated sugar
¼ cup (½ stick) butter, softened
2 eggs
1 teaspoon vanilla
1½ cups cake flour
1 teaspoon baking powder
¼ teaspoon baking soda
½ cup plain or vanilla yogurt
1 cup fresh blueberries
1 teaspoon all-purpose flour
1 cup chopped walnuts
½ cup packed brown sugar
1 teaspoon ground cinnamon

1. Preheat oven to 350°F. Line 8-inch square baking pan with foil and spray with nonstick cooking spray.

2. Beat applesauce, granulated sugar and butter in medium bowl with electric mixer at medium speed 2 minutes. Beat in eggs and vanilla. Sift cake flour, baking powder and baking soda into small bowl. Add to applesauce mixture with yogurt; beat until smooth. Toss berries with all-purpose flour and gently fold into batter.

3. Combine walnuts, brown sugar and cinnamon in small bowl. Pout half of batter into prepared pan. Sprinkle layer of walnut mixture over batter. Pour remaining batter over walnut mixture. Sprinkle remaining walnut mixture over top.

4. Bake 30 to 35 minutes or until toothpick inserted into center comes out clean. Cool completely on wire rack. Garnish as desired.

Makes 9 servings

Blueberry Yogurt Cake

Lemony Banana-Walnut Bread

⅔ **cup shortening**
1 **cup granulated sugar**
2 **eggs**
1½ **cups mashed ripe bananas (about 3 medium)**
7 **tablespoons fresh lemon juice (about 3 lemons), divided**
2 **cups all-purpose flour**
1 **teaspoon baking soda**
1 **teaspoon baking powder**
½ **teaspoon salt**
½ **cup chopped walnuts**
1 **tablespoon grated lemon peel**
½ **cup powdered sugar**

1. Preheat oven to 325°F. Grease 2 standard (8×4-inch) loaf pans.

2. Beat shortening and granulated sugar in large bowl with electric mixer at medium speed until well blended. Add eggs, 1 at a time, mixing well after each addition. Blend in bananas and 6 tablespoons lemon juice. Combine flour, baking soda, baking powder and salt in medium bowl. Add to banana mixture; mix until blended. Stir in walnuts and lemon peel. Pour evenly into prepared pans.

3. Bake 50 to 60 minutes until toothpick inserted into centers comes out clean. Remove from pans; cool completely on wire racks.

4. Combine powdered sugar and remaining 1 tablespoon lemon juice in small bowl; stir until smooth. Drizzle over cooled loaves.

Makes 2 loaves

Lemony Banana-Walnut Bread

Toffee Crunch Muffins

1½ cups all-purpose flour
⅓ cup packed brown sugar
2 teaspoons baking powder
½ teaspoon baking soda
½ teaspoon salt
½ cup milk
½ cup sour cream
1 egg, beaten
3 tablespoons butter, melted
1 teaspoon vanilla
3 bars (1.4 ounces each) chocolate-covered toffee, chopped, divided

1. Preheat oven to 400°F. Grease 36 mini (1¾-inch) muffin pan cups or line with paper baking cups.

2. Combine flour, sugar, baking powder, baking soda and salt in large bowl. Combine milk, sour cream, egg, butter and vanilla in small bowl until well blended. Stir into flour mixture just until moistened. Fold in two thirds of toffee. Spoon batter into prepared muffin cups, filling almost full. Sprinkle evenly with remaining toffee.

3. Bake 16 to 18 minutes or until toothpick inserted into centers comes out clean. Remove from pans; cool on wire racks 10 minutes. Serve warm or cool completely.   *Makes 36 mini muffins*

Variation: For regular-size muffins, spoon batter into 10 standard (2½-inch) greased or paper-lined muffin cups. Bake at 350°F about 20 minutes or until toothpick inserted into centers comes out clean. Makes 10 muffins.

Toffee Crunch Muffins

Best-Selling Bars

Oatmeal Date Bars

> 2 packages (18 ounces each) refrigerated oatmeal raisin cookie
>   dough
> 2½ cups uncooked old-fashioned oats, divided
> 2 packages (8 ounces each) chopped dates
> 1 cup water
> ½ cup sugar
> 1 teaspoon vanilla

1. Let dough stand at room temperature about 15 minutes. Preheat oven to
350°F. Lightly grease 13×9-inch baking pan.

2. For topping, combine ¾ of one package of dough and 1 cup oats in
medium bowl. Beat until well blended; set aside.

3. For crust, combine remaining 1¼ packages dough and remaining 1½ cups
oats in large bowl; beat until well blended. Press dough evenly onto bottom
of prepared pan. Bake 10 minutes.

4. For filling, combine dates, water and sugar in medium saucepan; bring to
a boil over high heat. Boil 3 minutes; remove from heat and stir in vanilla.
Spread date mixture evenly over partially baked crust; sprinkle evenly with
topping mixture. Bake 25 to 28 minutes or until filling is bubbly. Cool
completely in pan on wire rack. *Makes about 2 dozen bars*

*Clockwise from top left: Oatmeal Date Bars,
Peanut Butter and Milk Chocolate Chip Brownie
Bars (page 70), Taffy Apple Bars (page 71) and
Buried Cherry Bars (page 71).*

Tangy Lime Bars

1 package (18 ounces) refrigerated sugar cookie dough
¾ cup all-purpose flour, divided
1¼ cups granulated sugar
4 eggs
½ cup bottled key lime juice
1 drop green food coloring
1 teaspoon baking powder
   Powdered sugar

1. Preheat oven to 350°F. Let dough stand at room temperature about 15 minutes. Lightly grease 13×9-inch baking pan.

2. Combine dough and ½ cup flour in large bowl; beat until well blended. Press dough evenly onto bottom and ½ inch up sides of prepared pan. Bake 20 minutes.

3. Meanwhile, combine remaining ¼ cup flour, granulated sugar, eggs, juice, food coloring and baking powder in large bowl; beat until well blended.

4. Pour over baked crust. Bake 18 to 21 minutes or until edges are brown and center is just set. Cool completely in pan on wire rack. Sprinkle with powdered sugar just before serving. Store leftovers covered in refrigerator.

Makes 2 dozen bars

Double Chocolate Chewies

1 package DUNCAN HINES® Moist Deluxe® Butter Recipe Fudge
   Cake Mix
2 eggs
½ cup (1 stick) butter or margarine, melted
1 package (6 ounces) semisweet chocolate chips
1 cup chopped nuts
   Confectioners' sugar (optional)

1. Preheat oven to 350°F. Grease bottom only of 13×9×2-inch baking pan.

2. Combine cake mix, eggs and melted butter in large bowl. Stir until thoroughly blended. (Mixture will be stiff.) Stir in chocolate chips and nuts. Press mixture evenly into prepared pan. Bake at 350°F for 25 to 30 minutes or until toothpick inserted in center comes out clean. *Do not overbake.* Cool completely. Cut into bars. Dust with confectioners' sugar, if desired.

Makes 36 bars

Tangy Lime Bars

Chocolate Toffee Gems

2½ **cups all-purpose flour**
1½ **teaspoons baking soda**
 ¾ **teaspoon salt**
 1 **cup (2 sticks) unsalted butter, softened**
 ¾ **cup firmly packed light brown sugar**
 ⅓ **cup granulated sugar**
 2 **eggs, lightly beaten**
 2 **teaspoons vanilla**
 1 **package (10 ounces) toffee baking bits, divided**
 ½ **cup sweetened condensed milk (not evaporated)**
1½ **cups semisweet chocolate chips**

1. Preheat oven to 350°F. Grease 13×9-inch baking pan. Sift flour, baking soda and salt into medium bowl; set aside.

2. Beat butter and sugars in large bowl with electric mixer at medium speed until creamy. Add eggs and vanilla; beat until smooth. Gradually stir in flour mixture. Reserve ¼ cup toffee baking bits; stir remaining toffee bits into batter. Spread in prepared baking pan. Bake 35 to 40 minutes. Cool completely in pan on wire rack.

3. Combine sweetened condensed milk and chocolate chips in small saucepan. Cook and stir over low heat until chips are melted. Spread chocolate mixture over bars; sprinkle with reserved toffee bits. Let stand until set; cut into 1-inch squares. *Makes 3 dozen squares*

Chocolate Toffee Gems

Dusty Apricot Bars

1 package (12 ounces) white chocolate chips
⅓ cup butter
2 cups graham cracker crumbs
1 cup chopped pecans
2 cans (12 ounces each) apricot pastry filling
1 cup sweetened flaked coconut, plus additional for garnish

1. Preheat oven to 350°F. Grease 13×9-inch baking pan. Combine white chocolate chips and butter in medium saucepan; cook and stir over low heat until smooth. Stir in graham cracker crumbs and pecans. Let cool 5 minutes.

2. Press half of crumb mixture into prepared pan. Bake 10 minutes or until golden brown. Spread apricot filling evenly over crust. Combine coconut with remaining crumb mixture; sprinkle evenly over apricot filling.

3. Bake 20 to 25 minutes or until light golden brown. Cool completely in pan on wire rack. Sprinkle with additional coconut; cut into bars.

Makes 1½ dozen bars

Colorful Caramel Bites

1 cup plus 6 tablespoons all-purpose flour, divided
1 cup quick-cooking or old-fashioned oats, uncooked
¾ cup firmly packed light brown sugar
½ teaspoon baking soda
¼ teaspoon salt
¾ cup (1½ sticks) butter or margarine, melted
1¾ cups "M&M's"® Semi-Sweet Chocolate Mini Baking Bits, divided
1½ cups chopped pecans, divided
1 jar (12 ounces) caramel ice cream topping

Preheat oven to 350°F. Combine 1 cup flour, oats, sugar, baking soda and salt; blend in melted butter to form crumbly mixture. Press half the crumb mixture onto bottom of 9×9×2-inch baking pan; bake 10 minutes. Sprinkle with 1 cup "M&M's"® Semi-Sweet Chocolate Mini Baking Bits and 1 cup nuts. Blend remaining 6 tablespoons flour with caramel topping; pour over top. Combine remaining crumb mixture, remaining ¾ cup "M&M's"® Semi-Sweet Chocolate Mini Baking Bits and remaining ½ cup nuts; sprinkle over caramel layer. Bake 20 to 25 minutes or until golden brown. Cool completely. Cut into squares.

Makes 36 bars

Dusty Apricot Bars

Chocolate-Topped Peanut Bars

Bar Cookie Crust (recipe follows)
⅓ cup packed brown sugar
⅓ cup KARO® Light Corn Syrup
3 tablespoons margarine or butter
¼ cup heavy or whipping cream
1½ cups cocktail or dry roasted peanuts
1 teaspoon vanilla
⅓ cup (2 ounces) semisweet chocolate chips

1. Preheat oven to 350°F. Prepare Bar Cookie Crust according to recipe directions.

2. Meanwhile, for filling, in heavy 2-quart saucepan combine brown sugar, corn syrup, margarine and cream. Bring to boil over medium heat; remove from heat. Stir in peanuts and vanilla. Pour over hot crust; spread evenly.

3. Bake 10 to 12 minutes or until filling is set around edges and center is slightly firm. Remove pan to wire rack.

4. Sprinkle with chocolate chips; let stand 5 minutes. Spread chocolate randomly with tip of knife. Cool. Refrigerate 15 minutes to set chocolate. Cut into 2×1½-inch bars.   *Makes about 32 bars*

Prep Time: 30 minutes
Bake Time: 10 to 12 minutes

Bar Cookie Crust

MAZOLA NO STICK® Cooking Spray
2 cups flour
½ cup (1 stick) cold margarine or butter, cut into pieces
⅓ cup sugar
¼ teaspoon salt

1. Preheat oven to 350°F. Spray 13×9×2-inch baking pan with cooking spray.

2. In large bowl with mixer at medium speed, beat flour, margarine, sugar and salt until mixture resembles coarse crumbs. Press firmly into bottom and ¼ inch up sides of pan.

3. Bake 15 minutes or until golden brown. Top with filling. Finish baking according to individual recipe directions.   *Makes one crust*

Note: Can be prepared 1 day ahead.

Coconut Raspberry Bars

2 cups graham cracker crumbs
½ cup (1 stick) butter, melted
1⅓ cups (3½-ounce can) flaked coconut
1 can (14 ounces) sweetened condensed milk
1 cup red raspberry jam or preserves
½ cup chopped pecans
½ cup semisweet chocolate chips
½ cup white chocolate chips

1. Preheat oven to 350°F.

2. Combine graham cracker crumbs and butter in medium bowl. Press evenly onto bottom of ungreased 13×9-inch baking pan. Sprinkle with coconut; pour sweetened condensed milk evenly over coconut.

3. Bake 20 to 25 minutes or until lightly browned; cool completely in pan on wire rack.

4. Spread jam over coconut layer; sprinkle with pecans. Refrigerate for 3 to 4 hours.

5. Place semisweet chocolate chips in small resealable food storage bag; seal bag. Microwave on HIGH 1 minute. Turn bag over; heat on HIGH at 30-second intervals until chocolate is melted. Knead bag until chocolate is smooth. Cut off very tiny corner of bag; drizzle chocolate onto jam layer. Melt white chocolate chips as directed for chocolate chips. Drizzle over top of chocolate layer to make lacy effect; chill until chocolate is set. Cut into bars. *Makes 3 to 3½ dozen bars*

Cappuccino Crunch Bars

1¾ cups all-purpose flour, sifted
1 teaspoon baking soda
1 teaspoon salt
½ teaspoon ground cinnamon
1 cup (2 sticks) butter, softened
1½ cups packed brown sugar
½ cup granulated sugar
2 eggs
2 teaspoons instant coffee granules or espresso powder, dissolved in
    1 tablespoon hot water and cooled to room temperature
2 teaspoons vanilla
1 teaspoon grated orange peel (optional)
1 cup white chocolate chips
1 cup chocolate-covered toffee baking bits

1. Preheat oven to 350°F. Grease 13×9-inch baking pan.

2. Combine flour, baking soda, salt and cinnamon in large bowl; set aside.

3. Beat butter and sugars in large bowl with electric mixer at medium speed until fluffy. Add eggs, one at a time, beating well after each addition. Add coffee mixture, vanilla and orange peel, if desired; beat well. Add flour mixture; beat until well blended. Stir in white chocolate chips and toffee bits.

4. Spread batter evenly in prepared pan. Bake 25 to 35 minutes or until golden brown. Cool completely in pan on wire rack; cut into bars.

Makes about 2½ dozen bars

Cappuccino Crunch Bars

Chocolate Orange Gems

⅔ **cup butter-flavored solid vegetable shortening**
¾ **cup firmly packed light brown sugar**
 1 **large egg**
¼ **cup orange juice**
 1 **tablespoon grated orange zest**
2¼ **cups all-purpose flour**
½ **teaspoon baking powder**
½ **teaspoon baking soda**
½ **teaspoon salt**
1¾ **cups "M&M's"® Chocolate Mini Baking Bits**
 1 **cup coarsely chopped pecans**
⅓ **cup orange marmalade**
   Vanilla Glaze (recipe follows)

Preheat oven to 350°F. In large bowl, cream shortening and sugar until light and fluffy; beat in egg, orange juice and orange zest. In medium bowl, combine flour, baking powder, baking soda and salt; blend into creamed mixture. Stir in "M&M's"® Chocolate Mini Baking Bits and nuts. Reserve 1 cup dough; spread remaining dough in ungreased 13×9×2-inch baking pan. Spread marmalade evenly over top of dough to within ½ inch of edges. Drop reserved dough by teaspoonfuls randomly over marmalade. Bake 25 to 30 minutes or until light golden brown. *Do not overbake.* Cool completely; drizzle with Vanilla Glaze. Cut into bars. Store in tightly covered container.

Makes 24 bars

Vanilla Glaze: Combine 1 cup powdered sugar and 1 to 1½ tablespoons warm water until desired consistency. Place glaze in resealable plastic sandwich bag; seal bag. Cut a tiny piece off one corner of the bag (not more than ⅛ inch). Drizzle glaze over bars.

Chocolate Orange Gems

Luscious Lemon Bars

   2 cups all-purpose flour
   ½ cup powdered sugar, plus additional for dusting
   1 tablespoon plus 1 teaspoon grated lemon peel, divided
   ¼ teaspoon salt
   1 cup (2 sticks) cold butter, cut into small pieces
   1 cup granulated sugar
   3 eggs
   ⅓ cup fresh lemon juice

1. Preheat oven to 350°F. Grease 13×9-inch baking pan; set aside.

2. Combine flour, ½ cup powdered sugar, 1 teaspoon lemon peel and salt in large bowl. Cut in butter until mixture resembles coarse meal. Press mixture evenly into prepared baking pan. Bake 18 to 20 minutes or until golden brown.

3. Beat granulated sugar, eggs, lemon juice and remaining 1 tablespoon lemon peel in medium bowl with electric mixer at medium speed until well blended. Pour mixture evenly over warm crust. Bake 18 to 20 minutes or until center is set and edges are golden brown. Remove pan to wire rack; cool completely. Dust with sifted powdered sugar; cut into bars. Store leftovers covered in refrigerator. *Makes 3 dozen bars*

Coconut-Almond Mound Bars

   2 cups graham cracker crumbs
   ½ cup (1 stick) butter, softened
   ¼ cup powdered sugar
   2 cups flaked coconut
   1 can (14 ounces) sweetened condensed milk
   ½ cup whole blanched almonds
   1 cup (6 ounces) milk chocolate chips

Preheat oven to 350°F. Lightly grease 13×9-inch pan. Combine crumbs, butter and powdered sugar in large bowl until blended. Press onto bottom of prepared pan. Bake 10 to 12 minutes or until golden. Combine coconut and milk in small bowl; spread evenly over baked crust. Arrange almonds evenly over coconut mixture. Bake 15 to 18 minutes. Sprinkle chocolate chips over the top; allow chips to melt before spreading evenly over bars. Cool completely in pan on wire rack. *Makes about 3 dozen bars*

Luscious Lemon Bars

Peanut Butter and Milk Chocolate Chip Brownie Bars

6 tablespoons butter or margarine, melted
1¼ cups sugar
2 teaspoons vanilla extract, divided
3 eggs, divided
1 cup plus 2 tablespoons all-purpose flour
⅓ cup HERSHEY'S® Cocoa
½ teaspoon baking powder
½ teaspoon salt
1 can (14 ounces) sweetened condensed milk (not evaporated milk)
½ cup REESE'S® Peanut Butter
1 cup HERSHEY'S® Milk Chocolate Chips, divided
1 cup REESE'S® Peanut Butter Chips, divided
¾ teaspoon shortening

1. Preheat oven to 350°F. Grease 13×9-inch baking pan. Stir together butter, sugar and 1 teaspoon vanilla in large bowl. Add 2 eggs; stir until blended. Stir together flour, cocoa, baking powder and salt. Add to egg mixture, stirring until blended. Spread in prepared pan. Bake 20 minutes.

2. Meanwhile, stir together sweetened condensed milk, peanut butter, remaining egg and remaining 1 teaspoon vanilla extract. Pour evenly over hot brownie. Set aside 1 tablespoon each milk chocolate chips and peanut butter chips; sprinkle remaining chips over peanut butter mixture. Return to oven; continue baking 20 to 25 minutes or until peanut butter layer is set and edges begin to brown. Cool completely in pan on wire rack.

3. Stir together remaining milk chocolate chips, remaining peanut butter chips and shortening in small microwave-safe bowl. Microwave at HIGH (100%) 30 seconds; stir. If necessary, microwave at HIGH an additional 15 seconds at a time, stirring after each heating, until chips are melted and mixture is smooth when stirred. Drizzle over top of bars. When drizzle is firm, cut into bars. Store loosely covered at room temperature.

Makes 24 to 36 bars

Taffy Apple Bars

1 package (18 ounces) refrigerated sugar cookie dough
1 package (18 ounces) refrigerated peanut butter cookie dough
½ cup all-purpose flour
2 large apples, cored, peeled and chopped (3½ to 4 cups)
1 cup chopped peanuts
⅓ cup caramel ice cream topping

1. Let both packages of dough stand at room temperature about 15 minutes. Preheat oven to 350°F. Lightly grease 13×9-inch baking pan.

2. Combine both doughs and flour in large bowl; beat until well blended. Press dough evenly onto bottom of prepared pan. Spoon apples evenly over dough; press down lightly. Sprinkle with peanuts.

3. Bake about 35 minutes or until edges are brown and center is sct. Cool completely in pan on wire rack. Drizzle with caramel topping.

Makes about 2 dozen bars

Buried Cherry Bars

1 jar (10 ounces) maraschino cherries
1 package (18¼ ounces) devil's food cake mix *without* pudding
   in the mix
1 cup (2 sticks) butter, melted
1 egg
½ teaspoon almond extract
1½ cups semisweet chocolate chips
¾ cup sweetened condensed milk
½ cup chopped pecans

1. Preheat oven to 350°F. Lightly grease 13×9-inch baking pan. Drain maraschino cherries, reserving 2 tablespoons juice. Cut cherries into quarters.

2. Combine cake mix, butter, egg and almond extract in large bowl; mix well. (Batter will be very thick.) Spread batter in prepared pan. Lightly press cherries into batter.

3. Combine chocolate chips and sweetened condensed milk in small saucepan. Cook over low heat, stirring constantly, until chocolate melts. Stir in reserved cherry juice. Spread over cherries in pan; sprinkle with pecans.

4. Bake 35 minutes or until almost set in center. Cool completely in pan on wire rack.

Makes 24 bars

Mississippi Mud Bars

¾ **cup packed brown sugar**
½ **cup (1 stick) butter, softened**
1 **egg**
1 **teaspoon vanilla**
½ **teaspoon baking soda**
¼ **teaspoon salt**
1 **cup plus 2 tablespoons all-purpose flour**
1 **cup (6 ounces) semisweet chocolate chips, divided**
1 **cup (6 ounces) white chocolate chips, divided**
½ **cup chopped walnuts or pecans**

1. Preheat oven to 375°F. Line 9-inch square pan with foil; grease foil. Beat sugar and butter in large bowl until well blended.

2. Beat in egg and vanilla until light and fluffy. Blend in baking soda and salt. Add flour, mixing until well blended. Stir in ⅔ cup semisweet chips, ⅔ cup white chips and nuts. Spread dough in prepared pan.

3. Bake 23 to 25 minutes or until center feels firm. (Do not overbake.) Remove from oven; sprinkle with remaining ⅓ cup semisweet chips and ⅓ cup white chips. Let stand until chips melt; spread evenly over bars to create marbled effect. Cool in pan on wire rack until chocolate is set.

Makes about 3 dozen bars

Helpful Hint

Try cutting bars into triangles. Start by cutting bars into squares and making a cut from corner to corner. Not only will they look fun, but you will also get twice as many pieces to sell.

Mississippi Mud Bars

Blast-Off Brownies

4 (1-ounce) squares unsweetened chocolate
¾ cup (1½ sticks) butter or margarine
2 cups sugar
1 cup flour
3 eggs
1 tablespoon TABASCO® brand Pepper Sauce
½ cup semisweet chocolate chips
½ cup walnuts, chopped

Preheat oven to 350°F. Grease 9×9-inch baking pan. Melt chocolate and butter in small saucepan over medium-low heat, stirring frequently. Combine sugar, flour, eggs, TABASCO® Sauce and melted chocolate mixture in large bowl until well blended. Stir in chocolate chips and walnuts. Spoon mixture into prepared pan. Bake 35 to 40 minutes or until toothpick inserted in center comes out clean. Cool in pan on wire rack.

Makes 16 brownies

Decadent Blonde Brownies

1½ cups all-purpose flour
1 teaspoon baking powder
½ teaspoon salt
¾ cup granulated sugar
¾ cup packed light brown sugar
½ cup (1 stick) butter, softened
2 eggs
2 teaspoons vanilla
1 package (10 ounces) semisweet chocolate chunks
1 jar (3½ ounces) macadamia nuts, coarsely chopped

1. Preheat oven to 350°F. Grease 13×9-inch baking pan. Combine flour, baking powder and salt in small bowl; set aside.

2. Beat granulated sugar, brown sugar and butter in large bowl with electric mixer at medium speed until light and fluffy. Beat in eggs and vanilla. Add flour mixture. Beat at low speed until well blended. Stir in chocolate chunks and macadamia nuts. Spread batter evenly in prepared pan. Bake 25 to 30 minutes or until golden brown. Cool completely in pan on wire rack. Cut into 3¼×1½-inch bars. *Makes 2 dozen brownies*

Blast-Off Brownies

Chewy Toffee Almond Bars

1 cup (2 sticks) butter, softened
½ cup sugar
2 cups all-purpose flour
1⅓ cups (8-ounce package) HEATH® BITS 'O BRICKLE® Almond
    Toffee Bits
¾ cup light corn syrup
1 cup sliced almonds, divided
¾ cup MOUNDS® Sweetened Coconut Flakes, divided

1. Heat oven to 350°F. Grease sides of 13×9×2-inch baking pan.

2. Beat butter and sugar with electric mixer on medium speed in large bowl until fluffy. Gradually add flour, beating until well blended. Press dough evenly into prepared pan. Bake 15 to 20 minutes or until edges are lightly browned.

3. Meanwhile, combine toffee bits and corn syrup in medium saucepan. Cook over medium heat, stirring constantly, until toffee is melted (about 10 to 12 minutes). Stir in ½ cup almonds and ½ cup coconut. Spread toffee mixture to within ¼ inch of edges of crust. Sprinkle remaining ½ cup almonds and remaining ¼ cup coconut over top.

4. Bake an additional 15 minutes or until bubbly. Cool completely in pan on wire rack. Cut into bars. *Makes 36 bars*

Classic Layer Bars

1½ cups graham cracker crumbs
½ cup (1 stick) butter, melted
1⅓ cups flaked coconut
1½ cups semisweet chocolate chunks or chips
1 cup chopped nuts
1 can (14 ounces) sweetened condensed milk

1. Preheat oven to 350°F. Combine graham cracker crumbs and butter in medium bowl; press mixture firmly onto bottom of 13×9-inch baking pan.

2. Sprinkle coconut, chocolate chunks and nuts over crumb layer. Pour sweetened condensed milk evenly over top. Bake 25 minutes or until golden brown. Cool completely on wire rack before cutting into bars.

Makes 3 dozen bars

Chewy Toffee Almond Bars

Peanutty Gooey Bars

Crust
- **2 cups chocolate graham cracker crumbs**
- **½ cup (1 stick) butter or margarine, melted**
- **⅓ cup granulated sugar**

Topping
- **1⅔ cups (11-ounce package) NESTLÉ® TOLL HOUSE® Peanut Butter & Milk Chocolate Morsels, *divided***
- **1 can (14 ounces) NESTLÉ® CARNATION® Sweetened Condensed Milk**
- **1 teaspoon vanilla extract**
- **1 cup coarsely chopped peanuts**

PREHEAT oven to 350°F.

For Crust
COMBINE graham cracker crumbs, butter and sugar in medium bowl; press onto bottom of ungreased 13×9-inch baking pan.

For Topping
MICROWAVE *1 cup* morsels, sweetened condensed milk and vanilla extract in medium, uncovered, microwave-safe bowl on HIGH (100%) power for 1 minute. Stir. Morsels may retain some of their original shape. If necessary, microwave at additional 10- to 15-second intervals, stirring until morsels are melted. Pour evenly over crust. Top with nuts and *remaining* morsels.

BAKE for 20 to 25 minutes or until edges are bubbly. Cool completely in pan on wire rack. Cut into bars.   *Makes 2 dozen bars*

Peanutty Gooey Bars

Blue-Ribbon Pies & Tarts

Apple Cranberry Streusel Custard Pie

1 (14-ounce) can EAGLE BRAND® Sweetened Condensed Milk
   (NOT evaporated milk)
1 teaspoon ground cinnamon
2 eggs, beaten
½ cup hot water
1½ cups fresh or dry-pack frozen cranberries
2 medium all-purpose apples, peeled and sliced (about 1½ cups)
1 (9-inch) unbaked pie crust
½ cup firmly packed light brown sugar
½ cup all-purpose flour
¼ cup (½ stick) butter or margarine, softened
½ cup chopped nuts

1. Place rack in lower third of oven; preheat oven to 425°F. In large bowl, combine EAGLE BRAND® and cinnamon. Add eggs, water and fruits; mix well. Pour into crust.

2. In medium bowl, combine brown sugar and flour; cut in butter until crumbly. Add nuts. Sprinkle over pie. Bake 10 minutes.

3. Reduce oven temperature to 375°F; continue baking 30 to 40 minutes or until golden brown. Cool. Store covered in refrigerator.

Makes one (9-inch) pie

Prep Time: 25 minutes
Bake Time: 40 to 50 minutes

Clockwise from top left: Apple Cranberry Streusel Custard Pie, Perfect Pumpkin Pie (page 96), Blueberry Pie (page 88) and Rhubarb Tart (page 88).

Autumn Pear Tart

    9-inch Tart Pastry (recipe follows)
  3 to 4 tablespoons sugar
  2 tablespoons cornstarch
  3 to 4 large pears, cut into halves, cored, pared and sliced
  1 tablespoon lemon juice
    Ground cinnamon (optional)
    Ground nutmeg (optional)
  ¼ cup apple jelly, warm

1. Preheat oven to 425°F. Roll out pastry on floured surface to ⅛-inch thickness. Ease pastry into 9-inch tart pan with removable bottom; trim edge. Pierce bottom of pastry with tines of fork; bake 15 to 20 minutes or until pastry begins to brown. Cool on wire rack.

2. Combine sugar and cornstarch in small bowl; mix well. Sprinkle pears with lemon juice; toss with sugar mixture. Arrange sliced pears on pastry. Sprinkle lightly with cinnamon and nutmeg, if desired.

3. Bake 20 to 30 minutes or until pears are tender and crust is browned. Cool on wire rack. Brush pears with warm jelly. Remove side of pan; place tart on serving plate. *Makes 8 servings*

9-inch Tart Pastry

  1⅓ cups cake flour
    2 tablespoons sugar
    ¼ teaspoon salt
    ¼ cup shortening
    4 to 5 tablespoons ice water

Combine flour, sugar and salt in small bowl. Cut in shortening with pastry blender or 2 knives until mixture forms coarse crumbs. Mix in ice water, 1 tablespoon at a time, until mixture comes together and forms a soft dough. Wrap in plastic wrap. Refrigerate 30 minutes before using.

Makes pastry for one (9-inch) tart

Autumn Pear Tart

Fudge Brownie Pie

  2 eggs
  1 cup sugar
  ½ cup (1 stick) butter or margarine, melted
  ½ cup all-purpose flour
  ⅓ cup HERSHEY'S Cocoa
  ¼ teaspoon salt
  1 teaspoon vanilla extract
  ½ cup chopped nuts (optional)
     Ice cream
     Hot Fudge Sauce (recipe follows)

1. Heat oven to 350°F. Lightly grease 8-inch pie plate.

2. Beat eggs in small bowl; blend in sugar and melted butter. Stir together flour, cocoa and salt; add to butter mixture. Stir in vanilla and nuts, if desired. Pour into prepared pie plate.

3. Bake 25 to 30 minutes or until almost set. (Pie will not test done in center.) Cool; cut into wedges. Serve topped with scoop of ice cream and drizzled with Hot Fudge Sauce. *Makes 6 to 8 servings*

Hot Fudge Sauce

  ¾ cup sugar
  ½ cup HERSHEY'S Cocoa
  ½ cup plus 2 tablespoons (5-ounce can) evaporated milk
  ⅓ cup light corn syrup
  ⅓ cup butter or margarine
  1 teaspoon vanilla extract

Stir together sugar and cocoa in small saucepan; blend in evaporated milk and corn syrup. Cook over medium heat, stirring constantly, until mixture boils; boil and stir 1 minute. Remove from heat; stir in butter and vanilla. Serve warm. *Makes about 1¾ cups sauce*

Fudge Brownie Pie

Apple-Cheddar Tart

Cheddar Pastry (recipe follows)
1 egg white
6 cups sliced peeled apples
2 teaspoons ground cinnamon
¼ teaspoon ground nutmeg
½ cup thawed frozen unsweetened apple juice concentrate
2 tablespoons cornstarch
2 tablespoons butter or margarine
Sharp Cheddar cheese, sliced (optional)

1. Preheat oven to 400°F. Prepare Cheddar Pastry. Roll out pastry dough to 12-inch circle. Place in 10-inch tart pan with removable bottom or 10-inch quiche dish; trim pastry and flute edges, sealing to side of pan. Prick bottom and sides of pastry with fork. Beat egg white until frothy; brush lightly over bottom of pastry. Bake 15 minutes. *Reduce oven temperature to 350°F.*

2. Place apples in large bowl. Add cinnamon and nutmeg; toss lightly to coat. Combine apple juice concentrate and cornstarch; mix well. Add to apple mixture; mix lightly. Spoon into partially baked crust; dot with butter. Bake 35 to 40 minutes or until apples are tender and crust is golden brown. Cool on wire rack. Serve with Cheddar cheese, if desired.

Makes 8 servings

Cheddar Pastry

1½ cups all-purpose flour
⅓ cup (1½ ounces) shredded sharp Cheddar cheese
¼ teaspoon salt
½ cup cold butter or margarine
3 to 4 tablespoons ice water

Combine flour, cheese and salt in medium bowl. Cut in butter with pastry blender or two knives until mixture forms coarse crumbs. Add water, 1 tablespoon at a time, mixing just until mixture forms dough; wrap in plastic wrap. Refrigerate 1 hour. *Makes pastry for one (10-inch) tart*

Apple-Cheddar Tart

Blueberry Pie

**6 cups fresh *or* 2 packages (16 ounces each) frozen unsweetened
    blueberries**
3 tablespoons lemon juice
1 cup plus 2 tablespoons EQUAL® SPOONFUL*
6 tablespoons cornstarch
    Pastry for double-crust 9-inch pie

*May substitute 27 packets EQUAL® sweetener.

• Toss blueberries and lemon juice in large bowl. Sprinkle with combined
Equal® and cornstarch; toss to coat. (If frozen blueberries are used, let stand
30 minutes.)

• Roll half of pastry on lightly floured surface into circle 1 inch larger than
inverted 9-inch pie pan. Ease pastry into pan; trim within 1 inch of edge of
pan. Roll remaining pastry to ⅛-inch thickness; cut into 10 to 12 strips,
½ inch wide.

• Pour blueberry mixture into pastry. Arrange pastry strips over filling and
weave into lattice design. Trim ends of lattice strips; fold edge of lower crust
over ends of lattice strips. Seal and flute edge.

• Bake in preheated 400°F oven 55 to 60 minutes or until pastry is browned
and filling is bubbly. Cover edge of crust with aluminum foil if browning too
quickly. Cool on wire rack; refrigerate leftovers.   *Makes 8 servings*

Rhubarb Tart

    Pastry for single-crust 9-inch pie
  4 cups sliced (½-inch pieces) fresh rhubarb
1¼ cups sugar
  ¼ cup all-purpose flour
  2 tablespoons butter, cut into chunks
  ¼ cup uncooked old-fashioned oats

1. Preheat oven to 450°F. Line 9-inch pie plate with pastry; set aside.

2. Combine rhubarb, sugar and flour in medium bowl; place in pie crust. Top
with butter. Sprinkle with oats.

3. Bake 10 minutes. *Reduce oven temperature to 350°F.* Bake 40 minutes
more or until bubbly.   *Makes 8 servings*

Provençal Apple-Walnut Crumb Pie

5 cups peeled and thinly sliced Red Delicious apples
1 tablespoon lemon juice
¾ teaspoon vanilla
½ cup packed dark brown sugar
⅓ cup plus 3 tablespoons all-purpose flour, divided
1 teaspoon ground cinnamon
¼ teaspoon ground nutmeg
1 frozen pie crust
¼ cup chopped walnuts
2 tablespoons granulated sugar
2 tablespoons cold butter, cut into small pieces

1. Preheat oven to 425°F. Place baking sheet in oven while preheating.

2. Combine apples, lemon juice and vanilla in large bowl; set aside.

3. Combine brown sugar, 3 tablespoons flour, cinnamon and nutmeg in medium bowl; blend thoroughly. Add brown sugar mixture to apple mixture; toss to coat. Spoon into pie crust; set aside.

4. Heat 10-inch nonstick skillet over medium-high heat. Cook walnuts 2 minutes, stirring constantly with wooden spoon until lightly browned and fragrant. Remove from heat; set aside.

5. Combine remaining ⅓ cup flour and granulated sugar in small bowl. Cut in butter using pastry blender or two knives until mixture resembles coarse crumbs; sprinkle evenly over pie. Top with walnuts.

6. Bake 35 to 40 minutes or until bubbly and apples are tender in center.

Makes 8 servings

Sweet Potato Pecan Pie

1 (9-inch) prepared deep-dish pie crust
1½ cups pecan halves
½ cup light corn syrup
1 egg white
2 cups cooked, puréed sweet potatoes (about 1½ pounds potato, uncooked)
⅓ cup brown sugar
½ teaspoon cinnamon
⅛ teaspoon ground nutmeg
⅛ teaspoon ground cloves
1 teaspoon vanilla
¼ teaspoon salt
2 eggs, beaten

1. Preheat oven to 400°F. With a fork, prick holes in the bottom of the pie shell. Bake about 10 minutes or until very lightly browned and dry; remove from oven. Reduce oven temperature to 350°F.

2. In a small bowl, stir the pecans, corn syrup and egg white together. Set aside.

3. In a large bowl, combine the purée, brown sugar, spices, vanilla and salt. Mix well. Fold in the beaten eggs.

4. Spread the sweet potato mixture in the baked pie crust. Spoon pecan mixture evenly over top. Bake 45 to 50 minutes or until pie is puffed up and topping is golden. Cool completely before serving.   *Makes 8 servings*

Helpful Hint

Tip

When buying sweet potatoes, choose those that are small to medium sized with smooth, unbruised skins. They are high in fiber and contain vitamins A and C.

Sweet Potato Pecan Pie

Linzer Tart

¾ cup (1½ sticks) butter or margarine, softened
2 egg yolks
2 tablespoons thawed frozen unsweetened apple juice concentrate
2 teaspoons vanilla
1 cup all-purpose flour
½ teaspoon baking powder
¼ teaspoon salt
¼ teaspoon ground cinnamon
⅛ teaspoon ground allspice
1½ cups ground blanched almonds *or* hazelnuts (about 8 ounces)
1 jar (10 ounces) raspberry fruit spread (about 1 cup)

1. Beat butter in large bowl until light and fluffy. Blend in egg yolks, apple juice concentrate and vanilla. Combine flour, baking powder, salt, cinnamon and allspice; mix well. Stir in almonds. Gradually add to butter mixture, mixing until well blended.

2. Spread 1½ cups batter evenly onto bottom of 10-inch tart pan with removable bottom or 10-inch springform pan. Spread fruit spread evenly over batter, leaving 1-inch border around edge. Spoon remaining batter into pastry bag fitted with ½-inch plain or star tip. Pipe batter in lattice design over fruit spread. Chill 30 minutes.

3. Preheat oven to 350°F. Bake tart 35 minutes or until crust is golden brown and fruit spread is bubbly. Cool completely on wire rack. Serve at room temperature. *Makes 8 servings*

Linzer Tart

Chocolate Pecan Pie

1 cup sugar
⅓ cup HERSHEY'S Cocoa
3 eggs, lightly beaten
¾ cup light corn syrup
1 tablespoon butter or margarine, melted
1 teaspoon vanilla extract
1 cup pecan halves
1 unbaked (9-inch pie) crust
Whipped topping (optional)

1. Heat oven to 350°F.

2. Stir together sugar and cocoa in medium bowl. Add eggs, corn syrup, butter and vanilla; stir until well blended. Stir in pecans. Pour into unbaked pie crust.

3. Bake 60 minutes or until set. Remove to wire rack and cool completely. Garnish with whipped topping, if desired. *Makes 8 servings*

Country Peach Tart

Pastry for single-crust 9-inch pie
4 cups sliced, pitted, peeled fresh peaches or frozen peaches, thawed
½ cup EQUAL® SPOONFUL*
1 tablespoon all-purpose flour
½ teaspoon ground cinnamon
¼ teaspoon almond extract

May substitute 12 packets EQUAL® sweetener.

• Roll pastry on floured surface to 12-inch circle; transfer to ungreased baking sheet. Combine peaches, Equal®, flour, cinnamon and almond extract; toss gently until peaches are evenly coated with mixture.

• Arrange peach mixture over pastry, leaving 2-inch border around edge of pastry. Bring edge of pastry toward center, overlapping as necessary.

• Bake tart in preheated 425°F oven 25 to 30 minutes or until crust is golden brown and peaches are tender. Serve warm or at room temperature.
Makes 8 servings

Chocolate Pecan Pie

Perfect Pumpkin Pie

1 (15-ounce) can pumpkin (about 2 cups)
1 (14-ounce) can EAGLE BRAND® Sweetened Condensed Milk
   (NOT evaporated milk)
2 eggs
1 teaspoon ground cinnamon
½ teaspoon ground ginger
½ teaspoon ground nutmeg
½ teaspoon salt
1 (9-inch) unbaked pie crust

1. Preheat oven to 425°F. Whisk pumpkin, EAGLE BRAND®, eggs, spices and salt in medium bowl until smooth. Pour into crust. Bake 15 minutes.

2. Reduce oven temperature to 350°F and continue baking 35 to 40 minutes longer or until knife inserted 1 inch from crust comes out clean. Cool. Garnish as desired. Store leftovers covered in refrigerator.

Makes one (9-inch) pie

Sour Cream Topping: In medium bowl, combine 1½ cups sour cream, 2 tablespoons sugar and 1 teaspoon vanilla extract. After pie has baked 30 minutes at 350°F, spread mixture evenly over top; bake 10 minutes.

Streusel Topping: In medium bowl, combine ½ cup packed brown sugar and ½ cup all-purpose flour; cut in ¼ cup (½ stick) cold butter or margarine until crumbly. Stir in ¼ cup chopped nuts. After pie has baked 30 minutes at 350°F, sprinkle streusel evenly over top; bake 10 minutes.

Chocolate Glaze: In small saucepan over low heat, melt ½ cup semisweet chocolate chips and 1 teaspoon solid shortening. Drizzle or spread over top of baked pie.

Harvest Time Praline Apple and Cranberry Pie

1½ cups packed brown sugar, divided
½ cup WATKINS® Vanilla Dessert Mix
1½ teaspoon WATKINS® Ground Cinnamon
6 cups peeled and sliced tart green apples
1¾ cups fresh cranberries
2 tablespoons lemon juice
1 unbaked 9-inch pie crust
½ cup (1 stick) unsalted butter
2 tablespoons evaporated milk
1½ teaspoon WATKINS® Vanilla
½ teaspoon WATKINS® Caramel Extract
1 cup chopped walnuts

Preheat oven to 350°F. Combine ¾ cup brown sugar, dessert mix and cinnamon in large bowl. Add apples, cranberries and lemon juice; toss to coat. Spoon mixture into pie crust, mounding in center. Bake for about 1½ hours or until apples are tender. (Cover with foil during last 30 to 45 minutes to prevent overbrowning.) Transfer to wire rack; uncover and cool.

Melt butter with remaining ¾ cup brown sugar and milk in heavy skillet over low heat, stirring frequently. Increase heat to medium-high and bring to a simmer, stirring constantly. Remove from heat; stir in extracts, then walnuts. Pour mixture into medium bowl; let stand about 10 minutes or until slightly thickened and cooled, stirring occasionally. Spoon topping over pie, covering completely. Let stand about 30 minutes or until topping sets.

Makes 10 servings

Strawberry Rhubarb Pie

Pastry for double-crust 9-inch pie
4 cups sliced (1-inch pieces) fresh rhubarb
3 cups sliced fresh strawberries
1½ cups sugar
½ cup cornstarch
2 tablespoons quick-cooking tapioca
1 tablespoon grated lemon peel
¼ teaspoon ground allspice
1 egg, lightly beaten

1. Preheat oven to 425°F. Roll out half the pastry; place in 9-inch pie plate. Trim pastry; flute edges, sealing to edge of pie plate. Set aside.

2. Place fruit in large bowl. Combine sugar, cornstarch, tapioca, lemon peel and allspice in medium bowl; mix well. Sprinkle sugar mixture over fruit; toss to coat well. Fill pie shell evenly with fruit. (Do not mound in center.)

3. Roll out remaining pastry to 10-inch circle. Cut into ½-inch-wide strips. Arrange in lattice design over fruit. Brush egg over pastry.

4. Bake 50 minutes or until filling is thick and bubbly. Cool on wire rack. Serve warm or at room temperature.   *Makes 8 servings*

Helpful Hint

Tip

Fruit pies are always a hit at bake sales but they can also make a big mess in the oven. Juicy fillings often bubble over the sides of the pie pan, but placing the pie on a baking sheet before putting it in the oven helps to contain the mess and makes clean up easy as pie!

Strawberry Rhubarb Pie

Rustic Apple Croustade

1⅓ cups all-purpose flour
¼ teaspoon salt
2 tablespoons butter or margarine
2 tablespoons shortening
4 to 5 tablespoons ice water
⅓ cup packed light brown sugar
1 tablespoon cornstarch
1 teaspoon cinnamon, divided
3 large Jonathan or McIntosh apples, peeled, cored and
    thinly sliced (4 cups)
1 egg white, beaten
1 tablespoon granulated sugar

1. Combine flour and salt in small bowl. Cut in butter and shortening with pastry blender or two knives until mixture resembles coarse crumbs. Mix in ice water, 1 tablespoon at a time, until mixture comes together and forms a soft dough. Wrap in plastic wrap; refrigerate 30 minutes.

2. Preheat oven to 375°F. Roll out pastry on floured surface to ⅛-inch thickness. Cut into 12-inch circle. Transfer pastry to nonstick jelly-roll pan.

3. Combine brown sugar, cornstarch and ¾ teaspoon cinnamon in medium bowl; mix well. Add apples; toss well. Spoon apple mixture into center of pastry, leaving 1½-inch border. Fold pastry over apples, folding edges in gently and pressing down lightly. Brush egg white over pastry. Combine remaining ¼ teaspoon cinnamon and granulated sugar in small bowl; sprinkle evenly over tart.

4. Bake 35 to 40 minutes or until apples are tender and crust is golden brown. Let stand 20 minutes before serving. Cut into wedges.

Makes 8 servings

Rustic Apple Croustade

Blueberry Crumble Pie

1 (6-ounce) READY CRUST® Graham Cracker Pie Crust
1 egg yolk, beaten
1 (21-ounce) can blueberry pie filling
⅓ cup all-purpose flour
⅓ cup quick-cooking oats
¼ cup sugar
3 tablespoons margarine, melted

1. Preheat oven to 375°F. Brush bottom and sides of crust with egg yolk; bake on baking sheet 5 minutes or until light brown.

2. Pour blueberry pie filling into crust. Combine flour, oats and sugar in small bowl; mix in margarine. Spoon over pie filling.

3. Bake on baking sheet about 35 minutes or until filling is bubbly and topping is browned. Cool on wire rack. *Makes 8 servings*

Prep Time: 15 minutes
Bake Time: 40 minutes

All-American Cookie Pie

1 refrigerated pie crust (half of 15-ounce package)
¾ cup (1½ sticks) butter, softened
½ cup granulated sugar
½ cup packed brown sugar
½ teaspoon vanilla
2 eggs
¾ cup all-purpose flour
1 cup (6 ounces) semisweet chocolate chunks or chips
1 cup chopped nuts

1. Preheat oven to 325°F. Place crust in 9-inch pie pan; flute edge as desired.

2. Beat butter, granulated sugar, brown sugar and vanilla in large bowl with electric mixer at medium speed until light and fluffy. Add eggs; beat until well blended. Beat in flour just until blended. Stir in chocolate chunks and nuts. Spread evenly in crust.

3. Bake 65 to 70 minutes or until toothpick inserted into center comes out clean. Cool completely on wire rack. *Makes 8 servings*

Blueberry Crumble Pie

No-Bake Goodies

Cashew Macadamia Crunch

  2 cups (11.5 ounce package) HERSHEY'S Milk Chocolate Chips
  ¾ cup coarsely chopped salted or unsalted cashews
  ¾ cup coarsely chopped MAUNA LOA® Macadamia Nuts
  ½ cup (1 stick) butter, softened
  ½ cup sugar
  2 tablespoons light corn syrup

1. Line 9-inch square pan with foil, extending foil over edges of pan. Butter foil. Cover bottom of prepared pan with chocolate chips.

2. Combine cashews, macadamia nuts, butter, sugar and corn syrup in large heavy skillet; cook over low heat, stirring constantly, until butter is melted and sugar is dissolved. Increase heat to medium; cook, stirring constantly, until mixture begins to cling together and turns medium golden brown (about 10 minutes).

3. Pour mixture over chocolate chips in pan, spreading evenly. Cool. Refrigerate until chocolate is firm. Remove from pan; peel off foil. Break into pieces. Store tightly covered in cool, dry place.

Makes about 1½ pounds

Prep Time: 30 minutes
Cook Time: 10 minutes
Cool Time: 40 minutes
Chill Time: 3 hours

Clockwise from top left: Cashew Macadamia Crunch, Fluted Kisses® Cups with Peanut Butter Filling (page 112), Candy Crunch (page 112) and Coconut Bonbons (page 122).

No-Bake Chocolate Peanut Butter Bars

2 cups peanut butter, *divided*
¾ cup (1½ sticks) butter, softened
2 cups powdered sugar
3 cups graham cracker crumbs
**2 cups (12-ounce package) NESTLÉ® TOLL HOUSE® Semi-Sweet
    Chocolate Mini Morsels,** *divided*

GREASE 13×9-inch baking pan.

BEAT *1¼* cups peanut butter and butter in large mixer bowl until creamy. Gradually beat in *1 cup* powdered sugar. With hands or wooden spoon, work in *remaining* powdered sugar, graham cracker crumbs and *½ cup* morsels. Press evenly into prepared pan. Smooth top with spatula.

MELT *remaining* peanut butter and *remaining* morsels in medium, *heavy-duty* saucepan over *lowest possible heat,* stirring constantly, until smooth. Spread over graham cracker crust in pan. Refrigerate for at least 1 hour or until chocolate is firm; cut into bars. Store in refrigerator.

Makes 5 dozen bars

Crispy Bites

2 tablespoons unsalted butter, softened
¼ teaspoon salt
3 cups mini marshmallows
3 cups crisped rice cereal
1 cup semisweet chocolate chips
2 teaspoons canola or vegetable oil

1. Melt butter over medium-low heat in large heavy-bottomed pot. Stir in salt. Add marshmallows, stirring constantly until melted. Remove from heat and add cereal. Stir vigorously to combine. Set aside for 10 minutes or until mixture is cool enough to handle and loses some of its stickiness.

2. Dampen hands with water and shape cereal mixture into 1½-inch balls. Place on parchment paper. Set aside 1 hour or until the balls cool completely.

3. Melt chocolate in top of double boiler. Stir in oil. Using a fork, drizzle chocolate over the cereal balls. Set aside for 3 hours or refrigerate for 1 hour to allow chocolate to set.

Makes 4 dozen treats

No-Bake Chocolate Peanut Butter Bars

Caramel-Marshmallow Apples

1 package (14 ounces) caramels
1 cup miniature marshmallows
1 tablespoon water
5 or 6 small apples, rinsed and dried

1. Line baking sheet with buttered waxed paper; set aside.

2. Combine caramels, marshmallows and water in medium saucepan. Cook over medium heat, stirring constantly, until caramels melt. Cool slightly while preparing apples.

3. Insert flat sticks in stem ends of apples. Dip apples in caramel mixture, one at a time, coating completely. Remove excess caramel mixture by scraping apple bottoms across rim of saucepan. Place on prepared baking sheet. Refrigerate until firm. *Makes 5 or 6 apples*

Caramel-Nut Apples: Roll coated apples in chopped nuts before refrigerating.

Caramel-Chocolate Apples: Drizzle melted milk chocolate over coated apples before refrigerating.

Mint Truffles

1 package (10 ounces) mint chocolate chips
⅓ cup whipping cream
¼ cup (½ stick) butter or margarine
1 container (3½ ounces) chocolate sprinkles

1. Line baking sheet with waxed paper; set aside. Melt chips with whipping cream and butter in heavy medium saucepan over low heat, stirring occasionally. Pour into pie pan. Refrigerate until mixture is fudgy, about 2 hours.

2. Shape about 1 tablespoonful mixture into 1¼-inch ball; place on waxed paper. Repeat procedure with remaining mixture.

3. Place sprinkles in shallow bowl; roll balls in sprinkles. Place truffles in petit four or candy cups. (If sprinkles won't stick because truffle has set, roll truffle between palms until outside is soft.) Truffles may be refrigerated 2 to 3 days or frozen several weeks. *Makes about 24 truffles*

Clockwise from top right: Caramel-Nut Apple,
Caramel-Chocolate Apple and
Caramel-Marshmallow Apple

Peanut Butter Blocks

1 (14-ounce) can EAGLE BRAND® Sweetened Condensed Milk
   (NOT evaporated milk)
1¼ cups creamy peanut butter
⅓ cup water
1 tablespoon vanilla extract
½ teaspoon salt
1 cup cornstarch, sifted
1 pound vanilla-flavored candy coating*
2 cups peanuts, finely chopped

Also called confectionery coating or almond bark. If it is not available in your local supermarket, it can be purchased in candy specialty stores.

1. In heavy saucepan, combine EAGLE BRAND®, peanut butter, water, vanilla and salt; stir in cornstarch. Over medium heat, cook and stir until thickened and smooth.

2. Add candy coating; cook and stir until melted and smooth. Spread evenly in wax-paper-lined 9-inch square baking pan. Chill 2 hours or until firm. Cut into squares; roll firmly in peanuts to coat. Store covered at room temperature or in refrigerator. *Makes about 3 pounds*

Microwave Method: In 1-quart glass measure, combine EAGLE BRAND®, peanut butter, water, vanilla and salt; stir in cornstarch. Microwave at HIGH (100% power) 2 minutes; mix well. In 2-quart glass measure, melt candy coating at MEDIUM (50% power) 3 to 5 minutes, stirring after each minute. Add peanut butter mixture; mix well. Proceed as directed above.

Prep Time: 15 minutes
Chill Time: 2 hours

Peanut Butter Blocks

Fluted Kisses® Cups with Peanut Butter Filling

72 HERSHEY'S KISSES® Brand Milk Chocolates, divided
1 cup REESE'S® Creamy Peanut Butter
1 cup powdered sugar
1 tablespoon butter or margarine, softened

1. Line small baking cups (1¾ inches in diameter) with small paper bake cups. Remove wrappers from chocolates.

2. Place 48 chocolates in small microwave-safe bowl. Microwave at HIGH (100%) 1 minute or until chocolate is melted and smooth when stirred. Using small brush, coat inside of paper cups with melted chocolate.

3. Refrigerate 20 minutes; reapply melted chocolate to any thin spots. Refrigerate until firm, preferably overnight. Gently peel paper from chocolate cups.

4. Beat peanut butter, powdered sugar and butter with electric mixer on medium speed in small bowl until smooth. Spoon into chocolate cups. Before serving, top each cup with a chocolate piece. Cover; store cups in refrigerator. *Makes about 2 dozen pieces*

Candy Crunch

4 cups (half of 15-ounce bag) pretzel sticks or pretzel twists
4 cups (24 ounces) white chocolate chips
1 (14-ounce) can EAGLE BRAND® Sweetened Condensed Milk
   (NOT evaporated milk)
1 cup dried fruit, such as dried cranberries, raisins or mixed dried
   fruit bits

1. Line 15×10-inch baking pan with foil. Place pretzels in large bowl.

2. In large saucepan, over low heat, melt chips with EAGLE BRAND®. Cook and stir constantly until smooth. Pour over pretzels, stirring to coat.

3. Immediately spread mixture in prepared pan. Sprinkle with dried fruit; press down lightly with back of spoon. Chill 1 to 2 hours or until set. Break into chunks. Store loosely covered at room temperature.
Makes about 1¾ pounds

Prep Time: 10 minutes
Chill Time: 1 to 2 hours

Black Russian Truffles

8 ounces premium bittersweet chocolate, broken into 2-inch pieces
¼ cup whipping cream
2 tablespoons butter
3½ tablespoons coffee-flavored liqueur
1½ tablespoons vodka
1 cup chopped toasted walnuts*

*To toast walnuts, spread in single layer on ungreased baking sheet. Bake in preheated 350°F oven 8 to 10 minutes or until golden brown, stirring frequently.

1. Place chocolate in food processor; process until chocolate is chopped.

2. Combine cream and butter in glass measuring cup. Microwave on HIGH 1½ minutes or until butter is melted and cream begins to boil.

3. With food processor running, pour hot cream mixture through feed tube; process until chocolate melts. Add liqueur and vodka; process until blended. Pour chocolate mixture into medium bowl; cover with plastic wrap and refrigerate overnight.

4. Shape chocolate mixture into 1-inch balls. Roll in walnuts. Store in airtight container in refrigerator. Let stand at room temperature 2 to 3 hours before serving. *Makes about 2½ dozen truffles*

Brandy Truffles: Substitute 3½ tablespoons brandy for coffee-flavored liqueur and vodka; add to chocolate mixture in Step 3. In place of walnuts, roll truffles in 1 cup powdered sugar.

Hazelnut Truffles: Substitute 3½ tablespoons hazelnut-flavored liqueur and 1½ tablespoons gold tequila for coffee-flavored liqueur and vodka; add to chocolate mixture in Step 3. In place of walnuts, roll truffles in 1 cup chopped toasted hazelnuts.

Gift Idea: Place these truffles in petit fours or paper candy cups and stack them in decorative coffee, tea or espresso cups. Wrap each cup in cellophane and arrange in a basket with a bag of gourmet coffee and a bottle of liqueur.

Mocha No-Bake Cookies

   1 package (9 ounces) chocolate wafer cookies
   ⅓ cup light corn syrup
   ⅓ cup coffee-flavored liqueur
   1 cup finely chopped walnuts, toasted
   ¾ cup powdered sugar
   3 tablespoons unsweetened cocoa powder
      Chocolate-covered coffee beans

1. Break half of cookies in half; place in food processor. Process using on/off pulses until fine crumbs form. Transfer to small bowl. Repeat with remaining cookies. Combine corn syrup and liqueur in medium bowl; stir until well blended. Stir in crumbs and walnuts until well blended.

2. Combine powdered sugar and cocoa in small bowl. Add ½ cup cocoa mixture to cookie crumb mixture; stir until blended. Reserve remaining cocoa mixture for coating.

3. Shape dough into 1-inch balls with greased hands; place in container. Cover container; refrigerate at least 3 hours or up to 3 days before serving.

4. Roll each ball in reserved cocoa mixture to coat; transfer to plate. Garnish with chocolate-covered coffee beans.   *Makes about 3 dozen cookies*

Hershey's Premier White Chips Almond Fudge

   2 cups (12-ounce package) HERSHEY'S Premier White Chips
   ⅔ cup sweetened condensed milk (not evaporated milk)
   1½ cups coarsely chopped slivered almonds, toasted*
   ½ teaspoon vanilla extract

*To toast almonds: Spread almonds in even layer on cookie sheet. Bake at 350°F 8 to 10 minutes or until lightly browned, stirring occasionally; cool.

1. Line 8-inch square pan with foil, extending foil over edges of pan.

2. Melt white chips with sweetened condensed milk in medium saucepan over very low heat, stirring constantly until mixture is smooth. Remove from heat. Stir in almonds and vanilla. Spread into prepared pan.

3. Cover; refrigerate 2 hours or until firm. Use foil to lift fudge out of pan; peel off foil. Cut fudge into squares.   *Makes about 3 dozen pieces*

Mocha No-Bake Cookies

Chocolate & Peanut Butter Dipped Apples

10 to 12 medium apples, stems removed
10 to 12 wooden ice cream sticks
1 cup HERSHEY'S Semi-Sweet Chocolate Chips
1⅔ cups (10-ounce package) REESE'S® Peanut Butter Chips, divided
¼ cup plus 2 tablespoons shortening (do *not* use butter, margarine, spread or oil), divided

1. Line tray with wax paper. Wash apples; dry thoroughly. Insert wooden stick into stem end of each apple; place on prepared tray.

2. Place chocolate chips, ⅔ cup peanut butter chips and ¼ cup shortening in medium microwave-safe bowl. Microwave at HIGH (100%) 1 minute; stir. If necessary, microwave at HIGH an additional 30 seconds at a time, stirring after each heating, just until chips are melted when stirred. Dip bottom three fourths of each apple into mixture. Twirl and gently shake to remove excess; return to prepared tray.

3. Place remaining 1 cup peanut butter chips and remaining 2 tablespoons shortening in small microwave-safe bowl. Microwave at HIGH 30 seconds; stir. If necessary, microwave at HIGH an additional 15 seconds at a time, stirring after each heating, just until chips are melted when stirred. Spoon over top section of each apple, allowing to drip down sides. Store in refrigerator.   *Makes 10 to 12 coated apples*

Chocolate & Peanut Butter Dipped Apples

Tropical Sugarplums

½ cup white chocolate chips
¼ cup light corn syrup
½ cup chopped dates
¼ cup chopped maraschino cherries, well drained
1 teaspoon vanilla
¼ teaspoon rum extract
1¼ cups gingersnap cookie crumbs
   Flaked coconut

1. Combine white chocolate chips and corn syrup in large saucepan. Cook and stir over low heat until melted and smooth.

2. Stir in dates, cherries, vanilla and rum extract until well blended. Add gingersnaps; stir until well blended. (Mixture will be stiff.)

3. Shape mixture into ¾-inch balls; roll in coconut. Place in miniature paper candy cups, if desired. Serve immediately or let stand overnight to allow flavors to blend.   *Makes about 2 dozen candies*

Prep Time: 20 minutes

Honey-Ginger Bourbon Balls

1 cup gingersnap cookie crumbs
1¼ cups powdered sugar, divided
1 cup finely chopped pecans or walnuts
1 square (1 ounce) unsweetened chocolate
1½ tablespoons honey
¼ cup bourbon

Combine crumbs, 1 cup powdered sugar and pecans in large bowl. Combine chocolate and honey in small bowl in top of double boiler; stir until chocolate is melted. Blend in bourbon. Stir bourbon mixture into crumb mixture until well blended. Shape into 1-inch balls; roll in remaining ¼ cup powdered sugar. Refrigerate until firm.   *Makes about 4 dozen balls*

Note: These improve with aging. Store them in an airtight container in the refrigerator. They will keep several weeks, but are best after two to three days.

Tropical Sugarplums

Cheery Chocolate Animal Cookies

1⅔ cups (10-ounce package) REESE'S® Peanut Butter Chips
1 cup HERSHEY'S Semi-Sweet Chocolate Chips
2 tablespoons shortening (do *not* use butter, margarine, spread or oil)
1 package (20 ounces) chocolate sandwich cookies
1 package (11 ounces) animal crackers

1. Line trays or cookie sheets with wax paper.

2. Combine peanut butter chips, chocolate chips and shortening in 2-quart glass measuring cup with handle. Microwave at HIGH 1½ to 2 minutes or until chips are melted and mixture is smooth when stirred. Using fork, dip each cookie into melted chip mixture; gently tap fork on side of cup to remove excess chocolate.

3. Place coated cookies on prepared trays; top each cookie with an animal cracker. Chill until chocolate is set, about 30 minutes. Store in airtight container in a cool, dry place.　　　　*Makes about 4 dozen cookies*

Creamy Caramels

½ cup slivered or chopped toasted almonds (optional)
1 cup (2 sticks) butter or margarine, cut into small pieces
1 can (14 ounces) sweetened condensed milk
2 cups sugar
1 cup light corn syrup
1½ teaspoons vanilla

1. Line 8-inch square baking pan with foil, extending edges over sides of pan. Lightly grease foil; sprinkle almonds over bottom of pan, if desired.

2. Melt butter in heavy 2-quart saucepan over low heat. Add sweetened condensed milk, sugar and corn syrup. Stir over low heat until sugar is dissolved and mixture comes to a boil. Carefully clip candy thermometer to side of pan. (Do not let bulb touch bottom of pan.) Cook over low heat about 30 minutes or until thermometer registers 240°F (soft-ball stage), stirring occasionally. Immediately remove from heat and stir in vanilla. Pour mixture into prepared pan. Cool completely.

3. Using foil, lift caramels out of pan; remove foil. Cut into 1-inch squares with sharp knife. Wrap each square in plastic wrap. Store in airtight container.　　　　*Makes about 2½ pounds or 64 caramels*

Cheery Chocolate Animal Cookies

Coconut Bonbons

2 cups powdered sugar
1 cup flaked coconut
3 tablespoons evaporated milk
2 tablespoons butter, softened
1 teaspoon vanilla
1 cup (6 ounces) semisweet chocolate chips
1 tablespoon shortening
   Toasted coconut and/or melted white chocolate (optional)

1. Line baking sheet with waxed paper; set aside.

2. Combine powdered sugar, coconut, milk, butter and vanilla in medium bowl. Stir until well blended. Shape mixture into 1-inch balls; place on prepared baking sheet. Refrigerate until firm.

3. Combine chocolate chips and shortening in small microwavable bowl. Microwave on HIGH 1 minute; stir. Microwave at 30-second intervals, stirring after each interval, until chocolate is melted and mixture is smooth.

4. Dip bonbons in melted chocolate using toothpick or wooden skewer. Remove excess chocolate by scraping bottom of bonbon across bowl rim; return to prepared baking sheet. Sprinkle some bonbons with toasted coconut, if desired. Refrigerate all bonbons until firm. Drizzle plain bonbons with melted white chocolate, if desired. Store in refrigerator.

Makes about 3 dozen bonbons

Helpful Hint

For an artful display, place the bonbons in paper candy cups. Arrange some crinkled paper gift basket filler in the bottom of a tin or gift box and nestle a few candies in the filler.

Chocolate Peanut Clusters

½ cup **HERSHEY'S Milk Chocolate Chips**
½ cup **HERSHEY'S Semi-Sweet Chocolate Chips**
 1 tablespoon **shortening (do *not* use butter, margarine, spread or oil)**
 1 cup **unsalted, roasted peanuts**

1. Place milk chocolate chips, semi-sweet chocolate chips and shortening in small microwave-safe bowl. Microwave at HIGH (100%) 1 to 1½ minutes or just until chips are melted and mixture is smooth when stirred. Stir in peanuts.

2. Drop by teaspoons into 1-inch diameter candy or petit four papers. Allow to set until firm. Store in airtight container in cool, dry place.

Makes about 2 dozen candies

Monkey Bars

 3 cups **miniature marshmallows**
½ cup **honey**
⅓ cup **butter**
¼ cup **peanut butter**
 2 teaspoons **vanilla**
¼ teaspoon **salt**
 4 cups **crispy rice cereal**
 2 cups **rolled oats, uncooked**
½ cup **flaked coconut**
¼ cup **peanuts**

Combine marshmallows, honey, butter, peanut butter, vanilla and salt in medium saucepan. Melt marshmallow mixture over low heat, stirring constantly. Combine rice cereal, oats, coconut and peanuts in 13×9×2-inch baking pan. Pour marshmallow mixture over dry ingredients. Mix until thoroughly coated. Press mixture firmly into pan. Cool completely before cutting.

Makes 2 dozen bars

Microwave Directions: Microwave marshmallows, honey, butter, peanut butter, vanilla and salt in 2-quart microwave-safe bowl on HIGH 2½ to 3 minutes. Continue as above.

Favorite recipe from **National Honey Board**

Turtle Caramel Apples

4 large Golden Delicious or Granny Smith apples
4 craft sticks*
1 package (14 ounces) caramels
2 tablespoons water
2 jars (3½ ounces each) macadamia nuts or pecans, coarsely chopped
1 bittersweet or semisweet chocolate candy bar (about 2 ounces),
broken into small pieces

Available where cake decorating supplies are sold.

1. Line 13×9-inch baking pan with waxed paper; set aside. To prepare apples, wash and dry completely. Remove stems. Insert craft sticks into centers of apples.

2. Combine caramels and water in small saucepan. Simmer over low heat until caramels melt and mixture is smooth, stirring frequently.

3. Immediately dip apples, one at a time, into caramel to cover completely. Scrape excess caramel from bottom of apple onto side of saucepan, letting excess drip back into saucepan.

4. Immediately roll apples in nuts to lightly coat, pressing nuts lightly with fingers so they stick to caramel. Place apples, stick-side up, on prepared baking sheet. Let stand 20 minutes or until caramel is set.

5. Place chocolate in small resealable food storage bag; seal bag. Microwave on MEDIUM (50%) 1 minute. Turn bag over; microwave on MEDIUM 1 minute or until melted. Knead bag until chocolate is smooth. Cut off very tiny corner of bag; pipe or drizzle chocolate decoratively onto apples.

6. Let apples stand 30 minutes or until chocolate is set. Store loosely covered in refrigerator up to 3 days. Let stand at room temperature 15 minutes before serving.   *Makes 4 apples*

Turtle Caramel Apples

No-Bake Gingersnap Balls

20 gingersnap cookies (about 5 ounces)
3 tablespoons dark corn syrup
2 tablespoons creamy peanut butter
⅓ cup powdered sugar

1. Place cookies in large resealable food storage bag; crush finely with rolling pin or meat mallet.

2. Combine corn syrup and peanut butter in medium bowl. Add crushed gingersnaps; mix well. (Mixture should hold together without being sticky. If mixture is too dry, stir in additional 1 tablespoon corn syrup.)

3. Shape mixture into 24 (1-inch) balls; roll in powdered sugar.

Makes 2 dozen cookies

Peanut Butter Cups

2 cups (12 ounces) semisweet chocolate chips
1 cup (6 ounces) milk chocolate chips
1½ cups powdered sugar
1 cup crunchy or smooth peanut butter
½ cup vanilla wafer crumbs (about 11 wafers)
6 tablespoons butter or margarine, softened

1. Line 12 standard (2½-inch) muffin cups with double-thickness paper baking cups or foil cups.

2. Melt both chips in heavy, small saucepan over very low heat, stirring constantly. Spoon about 1 tablespoonful chocolate into each cup. With back of spoon, bring chocolate up side of each cup. Refrigerate until firm, about 20 minutes.

3. Combine sugar, peanut butter, crumbs and butter in medium bowl. Spoon 2 tablespoons peanut butter mixture into each chocolate cup. Spread with small spatula.

4. Spoon about 1 tablespoon remaining chocolate over each peanut butter cup. Refrigerate until firm. *Makes 12 cups*

Note: To remove paper cups, cut slit in bottom of paper and peel paper up from bottom. Do not peel paper down from top edge.

No-Bake Gingersnap Balls

Toll House® Famous Fudge

1½ cups granulated sugar
⅔ cup (5 fluid-ounce can) NESTLÉ® CARNATION® Evaporated Milk
2 tablespoons butter or margarine
¼ teaspoon salt
2 cups miniature marshmallows
1½ cups (9 ounces) NESTLÉ® TOLL HOUSE® Semi-Sweet Chocolate
   Morsels
½ cup chopped pecans or walnuts (optional)
1 teaspoon vanilla extract

LINE 8-inch square baking pan with foil.

COMBINE sugar, evaporated milk, butter and salt in medium, *heavy-duty* saucepan. Bring to a *full rolling boil* over medium heat, stirring constantly. Boil, stirring constantly, for 4 to 5 minutes. Remove from heat.

STIR in marshmallows, morsels, nuts and vanilla extract. Stir vigorously for 1 minute or until marshmallows are melted. Pour into prepared baking pan; refrigerate for 2 hours or until firm. Lift from pan; remove foil. Cut into pieces.   *Makes 49 pieces*

For Milk Chocolate Fudge: SUBSTITUTE 1¾ cups (11.5-ounce package) NESTLÉ® TOLL HOUSE® Milk Chocolate Morsels for Semi-Sweet Morsels.

For Butterscotch Fudge: SUBSTITUTE 1⅔ cups (11-ounce package) NESTLÉ® TOLL HOUSE® Butterscotch Flavored Morsels for Semi-Sweet Morsels.

For Peanutty Chocolate Fudge: SUBSTITUTE 1⅔ cups (11-ounce package) NESTLÉ® TOLL HOUSE® Peanut Butter & Milk Chocolate Morsels for Semi-Sweet Morsels and ½ cup chopped peanuts for pecans or walnuts.

Toll House® Famous Fudge

Peanut Butter Truffles

2 cups (11½ ounces) milk chocolate chips
½ cup whipping cream
2 tablespoons butter
½ cup creamy peanut butter
¾ cup finely chopped peanuts

1. Combine chocolate chips, whipping cream and butter in heavy, medium saucepan; melt over low heat, stirring occasionally. Add peanut butter; stir until blended. Pour into pie pan. Refrigerate about 1 hour or until mixture is fudgy but soft, stirring occasionally.

2. Shape mixture by tablespoonfuls into 1¼-inch balls; place on waxed paper.

3. Place peanuts in shallow bowl. Roll balls in peanuts; place in petit four or paper candy cups. (If peanuts won't stick because truffle has set, roll truffle between palms until outside is soft.) Truffles can be refrigerated 2 to 3 days or frozen several weeks. *Makes about 36 truffles*

Tip: For a pretty contrast, roll some of the truffles in cocoa powder instead of chopped peanuts.

No-Bake Chocolate Oat Bars

1 cup (2 sticks) butter
½ cup packed brown sugar
1 teaspoon vanilla
3 cups uncooked quick oats
1 cup semisweet chocolate chips
½ cup crunchy or creamy peanut butter

1. Grease 9-inch square baking pan. Melt butter in large saucepan over medium heat. Add brown sugar and vanilla; mix well.

2. Stir in oats. Cook over low heat 2 to 3 minutes or until ingredients are well blended. Press half of mixture into prepared pan.

3. Melt chocolate chips in small heavy saucepan over low heat, stirring occasionally. Stir in peanut butter. Pour chocolate mixture over oat mixture in pan. Crumble remaining oat mixture over chocolate layer; press down gently. Cover and refrigerate 2 to 3 hours or overnight. Bring to room temperature before cutting into bars. *Makes 32 bars*

Peanut Butter Truffles

Year-Round Holiday Treats

Super-Lucky Cereal Treats

40 large marshmallows
¼ cup (½ stick) butter
6 cups oat cereal with marshmallow bits
Irish-themed candy cake decorations

1. Line 8-inch square pan with aluminum foil, leaving 2-inch overhang on 2 sides. Generously grease or spray with nonstick cooking spray.

2. Melt marshmallows and butter in medium saucepan over medium heat 3 minutes or until melted and smooth, stirring constantly. Remove from heat.

3. Add cereal; stir until completely coated. Spread in prepared pan; press evenly onto bottom using rubber spatula. Let cool 10 minutes. Using foil overhangs as handles, remove treats from pan. Cut into 16 bars. Press candy decorations onto top of treats. *Makes 16 treats*

Clockwise from top left: Super-Lucky Cereal Treats, Hanukkah Cookies (page 143), High-Flying Flags (page 140) and Autumn Leaves (page 142).

Quick Pumpkin Bread

1 cup packed light brown sugar
⅓ cup cold butter, cut into 5 pieces
2 eggs
1 cup solid-pack pumpkin
1½ cups all-purpose flour
½ cup whole wheat flour
1½ teaspoons pumpkin pie spice*
1 teaspoon baking soda
¾ teaspoon salt
½ teaspoon baking powder
¼ teaspoon ground cardamom (optional)
½ cup dark raisins or chopped, pitted dates
½ cup chopped pecans or walnuts

Substitute ¾ teaspoon ground cinnamon, ⅜ teaspoon ground ginger and scant ¼ teaspoon each ground allspice and ground nutmeg for 1½ teaspoons pumpkin pie spice.

1. Preheat oven to 350°F. Lightly grease 9×5-inch loaf pan or 3 mini 5×3-inch loaf pans. Fit processor with steel blade. Measure sugar and butter into work bowl. Process until smooth, about 10 seconds.

2. Turn on processor and add eggs one at a time through feed tube. Add pumpkin, flours, pie spice, baking soda, salt, baking powder and cardamom, if desired. Process just until flour is moistened, about 5 seconds. *Do not overprocess.* Batter should be lumpy.

3. Sprinkle raisins and nuts over batter. Process using on/off pulsing action 2 or 3 times or just until raisins and nuts are mixed into batter.

4. Turn batter into prepared loaf pan. Bake until toothpick inserted into center comes out clean, about 1 hour for larger loaf or 30 to 35 minutes for smaller loaves. Cool bread 15 minutes in pan. Remove from pan and cool on wire rack.   *Makes 1 large or 3 small loaves*

Note: Whole wheat flour can be omitted, if desired, and a total of 2 cups all-purpose flour used instead.

Quick Pumpkin Bread

Peppermint Patties

2 cups all-purpose flour
½ cup plus 1 tablespoon unsweetened cocoa powder, sifted, divided
1 teaspoon baking powder
½ teaspoon salt
¾ cup (1½ sticks) butter, softened
1 cup granulated sugar
1 egg
4 teaspoons vanilla, divided
1 to 1½ teaspoons peppermint extract
3 cups powdered sugar
4 tablespoons hot water or milk (not boiling)

1. Combine flour, ½ cup cocoa, baking powder and salt in small bowl; set aside. Beat butter and granulated sugar in large bowl with electric mixer at medium speed 1 minute or until creamy. Add egg, 1 teaspoon vanilla and peppermint extract; beat until well blended. Gradually stir in flour mixture just until blended.

2. On lightly floured work surface, shape dough into 12×2-inch log. Wrap tightly in waxed paper, then wrap in plastic wrap. Freeze 2 hours or until firm.

3. Preheat oven to 350°F. Grease cookie sheets. Cut dough into ⅛-inch slices. Place slices 1 inch apart on prepared cookie sheets. Bake 9 minutes or until puffed and firm to the touch. Cool on cookie sheets 1 to 2 minutes. Remove to wire rack; cool completely.

4. For icing, combine powdered sugar, hot water and remaining 3 teaspoons vanilla in medium bowl; stir until smooth. Add additional water, ½ teaspoon at a time, if necessary, until desired consistency is reached. Divide icing in half. Add remaining 1 tablespoon cocoa powder to one bowl; stir until well blended. Cover cocoa icing; set aside.

5. Frost cooled cookies with vanilla icing; let stand until set. Drizzle cookies with chocolate icing; let stand until set.   *Makes about 4 dozen cookies*

Peppermint Patties

I Think You're "Marbleous" Cupcakes

1 package (18¼ ounces) cake mix with pudding in mix (any flavor)
1¼ cups water
3 eggs
¼ cup vegetable oil
1 container (16 ounces) vanilla frosting
1 tube (4¼ ounces) red decorating icing

1. Preheat oven to 350°F. Grease 24 standard (2½-inch) muffin pan cups or line with paper baking cups.

2. Prepare cake mix according to package directions with water, eggs and oil. Spoon batter into prepared muffin cups, filling two-thirds full.

3. Bake 20 to 25 minutes or until toothpick inserted into centers comes out clean. Cool in pans on wire racks 20 minutes. Remove cupcakes to racks; cool completely.

4. Spread 1½ to 2 tablespoons frosting over each cupcake. Fit round decorating tip onto tube of icing. Squeeze 5 dots icing over each cupcake. Swirl toothpick through icing and frosting in continuous motion to make marbleized pattern or heart shapes.   *Makes 24 cupcakes*

Peppermint Chocolate Fudge

2 cups (12 ounces) milk chocolate chips
1 cup (6 ounces) semi-sweet chocolate chips
1 (14-ounce) can EAGLE BRAND® Sweetened Condensed Milk
     (NOT evaporated milk)
   Dash salt
½ teaspoon peppermint extract
¼ cup crushed hard peppermint candy

1. In heavy saucepan over low heat, melt chocolate chips with EAGLE BRAND® and salt. Remove from heat; stir in peppermint extract. Spread evenly in wax-paper-lined 8- or 9-inch square pan. Sprinkle with peppermint candy.

2. Chill 2 hours or until firm. Turn fudge onto cutting board; peel off paper and cut into squares. Store leftovers covered in refrigerator.
                         Makes about 2 pounds fudge

Prep Time: 10 minutes
Chill Time: 2 hours

I Think You're "Marbleous" Cupcakes

High-Flying Flags

¾ **cup (1½ sticks) unsalted butter, softened**
¼ **cup granulated sugar**
¼ **cup packed light brown sugar**
 1 **egg yolk**
1¾ **cups all-purpose flour**
¾ **teaspoon baking powder**
⅛ **teaspoon salt**
   **Lollipop sticks, blue and white decorating icing, white sugar stars
   and red string licorice**

1. Beat butter, sugars and egg yolk in medium bowl with electric mixer at medium speed until creamy. Add flour, baking powder and salt; beat until well blended. Wrap dough in plastic wrap and chill 1 hour or until firm.

2. Preheat oven to 350°F. Grease cookie sheets. Roll dough on lightly floured surface to ¼-inch thickness. Cut out dough using 3-inch flag-shaped cookie cutter. Place lollipop stick underneath left side of each flag; press gently to adhere. Place flags 2 inches apart on prepared cookie sheets.

3. Bake 8 to 10 minutes or until edges are lightly browned. Remove to wire racks; cool completely. Spread blue icing in square in upper left corner of each flag; arrange sugar stars on blue icing. Spread white icing over plain sections of cookies. Place strips of red licorice on white icing; allow to set.

Makes 3 dozen cookies

High-Flying Flags

Autumn Leaves

1½ cups (3 sticks) unsalted butter, softened
¾ cup packed light brown sugar
½ teaspoon vanilla
3½ cups all-purpose flour
1 teaspoon ground cinnamon
½ teaspoon salt
⅛ teaspoon ground ginger
⅛ teaspoon ground cloves
2 tablespoons unsweetened cocoa powder
Yellow, orange and red food colorings
⅓ cup semisweet chocolate chips

1. Beat butter, brown sugar and vanilla in large bowl with electric mixer at medium speed until light and fluffy. Add flour, cinnamon, salt, ginger and cloves; beat at low speed until well blended.

2. Divide dough into 5 equal sections. Stir cocoa into 1 section until well blended. (If dough is too dry and will not hold together, add 1 teaspoon water; beat until well blended and dough forms ball.) Stir yellow food coloring into 1 section until well blended and desired shade is reached. Repeat with 2 sections and orange and red food colorings. Leave remaining section plain.

3. Preheat oven to 350°F. Lightly grease cookie sheets. Working with half of each dough color, press colors together lightly. Roll dough on lightly floured surface to ¼-inch thickness. Cut dough with leaf-shaped cookie cutters of various shapes and sizes. Place cutouts 2 inches apart on prepared cookie sheets. Repeat with remaining dough sections and scraps.

4. Bake 10 to 15 minutes or until edges are lightly browned. Remove to wire racks; cool completely.

5. Place chocolate chips in small resealable food storage bag; seal. Microwave on HIGH 1 minute; knead bag lightly. Microwave on HIGH for additional 30-second intervals until chips are completely melted, kneading bag after each 30-second interval. Cut off tiny corner of bag. Pipe chocolate onto cookies in vein patterns. *Makes about 2 dozen cookies*

Hanukkah Cookies

½ cup (1 stick) unsalted butter, softened
1 package (3 ounces) cream cheese
½ cup sugar
¼ cup honey
1 egg
½ teaspoon vanilla
2½ cups all-purpose flour
⅓ cup finely ground walnuts
1 teaspoon baking powder
¼ teaspoon salt
    Blue, white and yellow decorating icings

1. Beat butter, cream cheese, sugar, honey, egg and vanilla in large bowl at medium speed of electric mixer until creamy. Stir in flour, walnuts, baking powder and salt until well blended. Form dough into ball; wrap in plastic wrap and flatten. Refrigerate about 2 hours or until firm.

2. Preheat oven to 350°F. Lightly grease cookie sheets. Roll out dough, working with one small portion at a time, to ¼-inch thickness on floured surface with lightly floured rolling pin. (Keep remaining dough wrapped in refrigerator.) Cut dough with 2½-inch dreidel-shaped cookie cutter and 6-pointed star cookie cutter. Place 2 inches apart on prepared cookie sheets.

3. Bake 8 to 10 minutes or until edges are lightly browned. Let cookies stand on cookie sheets 1 to 2 minutes. Remove to wire racks; cool completely. Decorate cookies as desired with blue, yellow and white icings.

Makes 3½ dozen cookies

Cobweb Cups

1 package (19.8 ounces) brownie mix, plus ingredients to
   prepare mix
½ cup mini semisweet chocolate chips
2 ounces cream cheese, softened
1 egg
2 tablespoons sugar
2 tablespoons all-purpose flour
¼ teaspoon vanilla

1. Preheat oven to 350°F. Line 18 standard (2½-inch) muffin cups with paper baking cups. Prepare brownie mix according to package directions for cakelike brownies. Stir in chocolate chips. Spoon batter into prepared muffin pans, dividing evenly.

2. Combine cream cheese and egg in small bowl; beat until well combined. Add sugar, flour and vanilla; beat until well combined.

3. Place cream cheese mixture in resealable food storage bag; seal bag. With scissors, snip off small corner from one side of bag. Pipe cream cheese mixture in concentric circle design on each cupcake; draw toothpick through cream cheese mixture, out from center, 6 to 8 times.

4. Bake 20 to 25 minutes or until toothpick inserted into centers comes out clean. Cool in pans on wire racks 15 minutes. Remove to racks; cool completely.   *Makes 18 cupcakes*

Helpful Hint

Tip

Using brownie and cake mixes is a great time saver. They allow you more time to think about decorating, making them perfect for creating beautiful treats for any school holiday party or seasonal bake sale.

Cobweb Cups

Easter Nest Cookies

1½ cups all-purpose flour
1 teaspoon baking powder
½ teaspoon salt
¾ cup (1½ sticks) butter
2 cups miniature marshmallows
½ cup sugar
1 egg white
1 teaspoon vanilla extract
½ teaspoon almond extract
3¾ cups MOUNDS® Sweetened Coconut Flakes, divided
   JOLLY RANCHER® Jelly Beans
   HERSHEY'S Candy-Coated Milk Chocolate Eggs

1. Heat oven to 375°F.

2. Stir together flour, baking powder and salt; set aside. Place butter and marshmallows in microwave-safe bowl. Microwave at HIGH (100%) 1 to 1½ minutes or just until mixture melts when stirred. Beat sugar, egg white, vanilla and almond extract in separate bowl; add melted butter mixture, beating until light and fluffy. Gradually add flour mixture, beating until blended. Stir in 2 cups coconut.

3. Shape dough into 1-inch balls; roll balls in remaining 1¾ cups coconut, tinting coconut, if desired.* Place balls on ungreased cookie sheet. Press thumb into center of each ball, creating shallow depression.

4. Bake 8 to 10 minutes or just until lightly browned. Place 1 to 3 jelly beans and milk chocolate eggs in center of each cookie. Transfer to wire rack; cool completely.   *Makes about 3½ dozen cookies*

*To tint coconut: Place ¾ teaspoon water and a few drops food color in small bowl; stir in 1¾ cups coconut. Toss with fork until evenly tinted; cover tightly.

Easter Nest Cookies

Hanukkah Coin Cookies

1 cup (2 sticks) butter or margarine, softened
1 cup sugar
1 egg
1 teaspoon vanilla extract
1¾ cups all-purpose flour
½ cup HERSHEY'S Cocoa
1½ teaspoons baking powder
½ teaspoon salt
    Buttercream Frosting (recipe follows)

1. Beat butter, sugar, egg and vanilla in large bowl until well blended. Stir together flour, cocoa, baking powder and salt; gradually add to butter mixture, beating until well blended. Divide dough in half; place each half on separate sheet of wax paper.

2. Shape each portion into log, about 7 inches long. Wrap each log in wax paper or plastic wrap. Refrigerate until firm, at least 8 hours.

3. Heat oven to 325°F. Cut logs into ¼-inch-thick slices. Place on ungreased cookie sheet.

4. Bake 8 to 10 minutes or until set. Cool slightly; remove from cookie sheet to wire rack. Cool completely. Prepare Buttercream Frosting; spread over tops of cookies. *Makes about 4½ dozen cookies*

Buttercream Frosting

¼ cup (½ stick) butter, softened
1½ cups powdered sugar
1 to 2 tablespoons milk
½ teaspoon vanilla extract
    Yellow food coloring

Beat butter until creamy. Gradually add powdered sugar and milk to butter, beating to desired consistency. Stir in vanilla and food coloring.

Makes about 1 cup frosting

Hanukkah Coin Cookies

Spooky French Silk Cream Tarts

Custard
- ½ **cup sugar**
- ½ **cup unsweetened cocoa**
- ⅓ **cup all-purpose flour**
- ¼ **teaspoon salt**
- 1¾ **cups whole milk**
- ⅔ **cup semisweet chocolate chips**
- 1 **cup whipped topping**

Crust
- 10 to 12 **mini graham cracker crusts**

Ghosts
- **Whipped topping**
- **Small round black candies or mini chocolate chips for eyes and chocolate sprinkles for mouth**

1. In a small saucepan, whisk together sugar, cocoa, flour and salt. Gradually whisk in milk. Place over medium-high heat and bring to a boil, whisking constantly, until a thick custard forms, about 1 to 2 minutes. (The custard can burn quickly, so whisk thoroughly and constantly.) Remove from heat. Stir in chocolate chips until melted and smooth. Pour custard into a bowl and cover with plastic wrap; plastic wrap should touch the surface of the custard to prevent skin from forming. Refrigerate until cold, or place bowl in larger bowl of ice and stir occasionally, being careful not to get water in the custard.

2. Add whipped topping to custard and whisk just until combined. Spoon custard into crusts (about ¼ cup per crust). Cover tarts with plastic wrap touching the custard and refrigerate at least 2 hours or overnight.

3. Before serving, form a ghost on top of the custard with dollops of whipped topping. Use candies to form eyes and mouth of ghost.

Makes 10 to 12 tarts

Spooky French Silk Cream Tarts

Patriotic Cocoa Cupcakes

2 cups sugar
1¾ cups all-purpose flour
¾ cup HERSHEY'S Cocoa
2 teaspoons baking soda
1 teaspoon baking powder
1 teaspoon salt
2 eggs
1 cup buttermilk or sour milk*
1 cup boiling water
½ cup vegetable oil
1 teaspoon vanilla extract
Vanilla Frosting (recipe follows)
Chocolate stars or blue and red decorating icings (in tube)

To sour milk: Use 1 tablespoon white vinegar plus milk to equal 1 cup.

1. Heat oven to 350°F. Grease and flour muffin cups (2½ inches in diameter) or line with paper bake cups.

2. Combine dry ingredients in large bowl. Add eggs, buttermilk, water, oil and vanilla; beat on medium speed of mixer 2 minutes (batter will be thin). Fill cups ⅔ full with batter.

3. Bake 15 minutes or until wooden pick inserted in centers comes out clean. Remove cupcakes from pan. Cool completely. To make chocolate stars for garnish, if desired, cut several cupcakes into ½-inch slices; cut out star shapes from cake slices. Frost remaining cupcakes. Garnish with chocolate stars or with blue and red decorating icing.

Makes about 30 cupcakes

Vanilla Frosting: Beat ¼ cup (½ stick) softened butter, ¼ cup shortening and 2 teaspoons vanilla extract in large bowl. Add 1 cup powdered sugar; beat until creamy. Add 3 cups powdered sugar alternately with 3 to 4 tablespoons milk, beating to spreading consistency. Makes about 2⅓ cups frosting.

Patriotic Cocoa Cupcakes

Holiday Peppermint Bark

2 cups (12-ounce package) NESTLÉ® TOLL HOUSE® Premier White Morsels
24 hard peppermint candies, unwrapped

LINE baking sheet with wax paper.

MICROWAVE morsels in medium, uncovered, microwave-safe bowl on MEDIUM-HIGH (70%) power for 1 minute. STIR. Morsels may retain some of their original shape. If necessary, microwave at additional 10- to 15-second intervals, stirring just until morsels are melted.

PLACE peppermint candies in *heavy-duty* resealable plastic food storage bag. Crush candies using rolling pin or other heavy object. While holding strainer over melted morsels, pour crushed candy into strainer. Shake to release all small candy pieces; reserve larger candy pieces. Stir morsel-peppermint mixture.

SPREAD mixture to desired thickness on prepared baking sheet. Sprinkle with reserved candy pieces; press in lightly. Let stand for about 1 hour or until firm. Break into pieces. Store in airtight container at room temperature.
Makes about 1 pound candy

Mom's Pumpkin Pie

1½ cans (15 ounces each) solid-pack pumpkin
1 can (12 ounces) evaporated milk
1 cup sugar
2 eggs
2 tablespoons maple syrup
1 teaspoon ground cinnamon
1 teaspoon vanilla
½ teaspoon salt
2 (9-inch) unbaked pie shells
Whipped cream (optional)

1. Preheat oven to 350°F. Combine all ingredients, except pie shells and whipped cream, in large bowl; mix well. Divide mixture evenly between pie shells.

2. Place pie pans on baking sheet. Bake 1 hour or until toothpick inserted into centers comes out clean. Cool completely. Top with whipped cream, if desired.
Makes 2 (9-inch) pies

Acknowledgments

The publisher would like to thank the companies
listed below for the use of their recipes
in this publication.

ACH Food Companies, Inc.

Cherry Marketing Institute

Duncan Hines® and Moist Deluxe® are registered trademarks of
Pinnacle Foods Corp.

EAGLE BRAND®

Equal® sweetener

The Hershey Company

Kellogg® Company

TM/© Mars, Incorporated 2007

McIlhenny Company (TABASCO® brand Pepper Sauce)

National Honey Board

Nestlé USA

The Sugar Association, Inc.

Watkins Incorporated

METRIC CONVERSION CHART

VOLUME MEASUREMENTS (dry)

$1/8$ teaspoon = 0.5 mL
$1/4$ teaspoon = 1 mL
$1/2$ teaspoon = 2 mL
$3/4$ teaspoon = 4 mL
1 teaspoon = 5 mL
1 tablespoon = 15 mL
2 tablespoons = 30 mL
$1/4$ cup = 60 mL
$1/3$ cup = 75 mL
$1/2$ cup = 125 mL
$2/3$ cup = 150 mL
$3/4$ cup = 175 mL
1 cup = 250 mL
2 cups = 1 pint = 500 mL
3 cups = 750 mL
4 cups = 1 quart = 1 L

VOLUME MEASUREMENTS (fluid)

1 fluid ounce (2 tablespoons) = 30 mL
4 fluid ounces ($1/2$ cup) = 125 mL
8 fluid ounces (1 cup) = 250 mL
12 fluid ounces ($1 1/2$ cups) = 375 mL
16 fluid ounces (2 cups) = 500 mL

WEIGHTS (mass)

$1/2$ ounce = 15 g
1 ounce = 30 g
3 ounces = 90 g
4 ounces = 120 g
8 ounces = 225 g
10 ounces = 285 g
12 ounces = 360 g
16 ounces = 1 pound = 450 g

DIMENSIONS

$1/16$ inch = 2 mm
$1/8$ inch = 3 mm
$1/4$ inch = 6 mm
$1/2$ inch = 1.5 cm
$3/4$ inch = 2 cm
1 inch = 2.5 cm

OVEN TEMPERATURES

250°F = 120°C
275°F = 140°C
300°F = 150°C
325°F = 160°C
350°F = 180°C
375°F = 190°C
400°F = 200°C
425°F = 220°C
450°F = 230°C

BAKING PAN SIZES

Utensil	Size in Inches/Quarts	Metric Volume	Size in Centimeters
Baking or Cake Pan (square or rectangular)	$8 \times 8 \times 2$	2 L	$20 \times 20 \times 5$
	$9 \times 9 \times 2$	2.5 L	$23 \times 23 \times 5$
	$12 \times 8 \times 2$	3 L	$30 \times 20 \times 5$
	$13 \times 9 \times 2$	3.5 L	$33 \times 23 \times 5$
Loaf Pan	$8 \times 4 \times 3$	1.5 L	$20 \times 10 \times 7$
	$9 \times 5 \times 3$	2 L	$23 \times 13 \times 7$
Round Layer Cake Pan	$8 \times 1 1/2$	1.2 L	20×4
	$9 \times 1 1/2$	1.5 L	23×4
Pie Plate	$8 \times 1 1/4$	750 mL	20×3
	$9 \times 1 1/4$	1 L	23×3
Baking Dish or Casserole	1 quart	1 L	—
	$1 1/2$ quart	1.5 L	—
	2 quart	2 L	—